Mastering the Game of
Life

Emerging From
The Forest

Paul D. Lowe

From Pain to Purpose

Dedication

For those that seek joy, rather than happiness...

For those that seek inspiration, rather than motivation...

For those that seek transformation, rather than change...

For those that seek awareness.

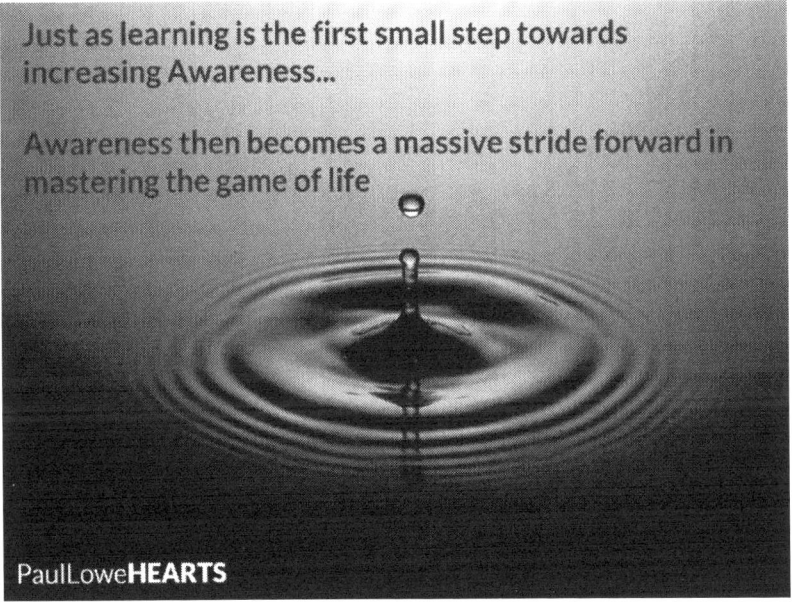

Praise

As Paul's coach and mentor, I know the benefits of his 'Three Pillars of Life' model can be life-changing. Paul's journey – from pain to prosperity – has been achieved by 'letting go' and he now uses his passion and drive to positively change other people's lives, globally.

JIM BRITT

Mentor and coach to Tony Robbins for five years |
Business partner with Jim Rohn for ten years | Leader in
the personal development industry for forty years |
Over a million attendees in seminars

Paul has applied his skills very successfully in helping and mentoring many people to get their lives back on track following setbacks, and he recently provided mentoring classes in Nottingham for groups of young footballers at Notts County Football Club. The feedback that I have been given from those who attended is that Paul's message has been an inspiration to them and one that aspiring young footballers should follow if they wish to achieve their goals.

LES BRADD

Notts County Football Club Ambassador |
All-time record goal-scorer for the club

Author's Note

Whether through the spoken or written word, my intention is consistently the same – to pass on life-enhancing insights to people; in the hope that I raise their awareness of how to achieve success in the game of life.

This particular book is the result of reflections on my previously published work; be that poems, short stories or books. In the case of the latter, there have been three other publications, with each one offering deeper insights than the previous version.

The first of the trio was self-published in 2000 – ironically called 'Mastering the Game of Life: Half-time Reflections' – and was essentially the foundation for the progression that has subsequently emerged.

My second account came some fifteen years later, when I was a co-author in 'The Change (9): Insights into Self-Empowerment'.

In 2017, I invited fifteen global co-authors to contribute to my own book 'Speaking From Our HEARTS: Mastering The Game of Life' – each story based upon real-life challenging experiences and how the individuals concerned overcame their respective pain and suffering.

Whether from the humble beginnings of that first self-publication nearly two decades ago, or the present-day's far more polished and professional product, I offer my utmost gratitude to be given the opportunity to serve others that seek improvement.

Just as I now have the awareness and acceptance to commit to my vocation of service, I truly acknowledge the multitude of people that have contributed towards my own development as a significant player within the game of life.

CONTENTS

Praise .... (i)

Author's Note .... (iii)

INTRODUCTION 1

PART ONE: FROM BLISS TO THE BEAST 3

PART TWO: THE BLACK & WHITE YEARS 31

PART THREE: LIVING LIFE ON PURPOSE 109

Epilogue: Reflections Of A Black & White Legend..... 129

Supporting HEARTS Global CIC 137

About The Author 139

INTRODUCTION

By sharing my journey from pain to purpose, I hope you gain a greater awareness of some of the key considerations that are required to achieve success in the game of life.

Whilst there is a strong reference to the influence of football – particularly in the early stages of my life – this story is not about 'The Beautiful Game' per se.

Similarly, with references to abuse, addiction and violence, the account is not specifically about any of these horrific experiences. Although these aspects offer a consistent thread throughout, the primary intention is to simply reach out and inspire those who are searching for their purpose in life.

So is the starting point pain? In a word – yes.

Pain is very subjective and presents itself in a variety of forms – spiritual, emotional, mental or physical – and unless our pain and suffering is sufficiently strong enough to want to instigate change, we will merely soldier on.

Do we not readily embrace clichés such as 'better the devil you know'? As humans, aren't we generally conditioned to 'just get on with it'?

Throughout my ensuing story, there are two really significant threads.

Firstly, the despicable behaviour of my step-father towards me and my mother; to the point where – at a very early age – I could no longer regard him as a human being and gave him a label of 'The Beast'.

Secondly, the resultant black and white existence that this created within my world; I subsequently began to experience life in this polarised way – there was never any grey in-between.

This stark account of my voyage is conveyed by equally graphic language, which I don't use today, but felt it necessary to include, giving my story the authenticity of where my life was at the time.

It is interspersed with Words of Wisdom (WOW); insightful thoughts which are based on my own experiences.

PART ONE:

FROM BLISS TO THE BEAST

'BAS-TAAAAAAAAAARDS!'

The shrill voice of a thirty-something man bellowed and challenged the sounds of the mercilessly beating rainfall as he emerged from the bridge holding his head. His fingers wiped sticky dark blood from a gash above his temple, and he stumbled briefly as he began to trot towards home.

It was a bleak wet winter's morning of mid-1960's inner-city Nottingham; the rain dripped heavily from the crevices of the seriously damaged brickwork of the old Marble Arch railway bridge on Bestwood Estate's border.

The bridge was a meeting place for the male youth of this typically gritty, 1940's council estate. For them, the favourite pass-time was to congregate on the top of the bridge and drop stones onto the heads of unsuspecting men that walked below – but only men, women and kids were never targeted. Even in those harsh days of survival, there was a moral code and honour amongst rogues.

The significance of Marble Arch was that it sandwiched – along with Andover Road – a triangular piece of glass-strewn ground that was surrounded by a small fence of railings, about a quarter the size of a conventional football pitch and provided the perfect opportunity for 'warm-up' activities such as stone-dropping, before the serious business of football got underway, especially if the kids got chased by the victims.

But this was not just any old piece of ground – no!

It was a mud bath that carried the hopes and dreams of most of the Bestwood lads that one day they would play for their beloved football team, whoever that might be.

The polarised reality was, either wear the red shirt of Nottingham Forest Football Club, or the rival black & white of Notts County Football Club – there were no other realistic alternatives.

During school hours, the numbers were few, except the die-hards that put their football education way ahead of learning the '3Rs' at school. Even then, there would typically be about a dozen kids that would converge on this hallowed ground – totally dedicated to learning their trade. They were very poor and these were hungry desperate days, so the key lesson being learnt at all times was the art of survival.

Not all the lads turned up to play football though. There were those that had no interest in playing football and chose instead, to display their sporting prowess in more of a boxing manner.

Opportunities for them to fight came regularly, especially when an opposition goal was scored or a misplaced tackle appeared. The football kids simply accepted it as being part of the game and part of everyday life on Bestwood.

'Shoot Paul!' Billy passionately demanded as I pulled back the trigger – that was my trusted right foot – ready to deliver an 'injury-time' winning goal.

A nearby street light stood like a weeping willow and offering a semblance of light as the evening darkness emerged.

'Fuckin' hell, how did you miss that?' Billy unsympathetically followed-up to me, his best mate as the ball rolled over a make-do goal-post, in the form of a jumper.

We were best mates – but only seemingly when needs were being met and on this occasion, I had failed miserably to meet those of Billy and my team-mates.

Billy was very tall and well-built, boasting a thick mop of dark wavy hair. His personality was very strong and straight-forward – a predictable character. His size gave him the confidence to strongly assert himself, although he certainly wasn't a bully.

As a seven-year-old, I was a wiry, athletic-type, with a dark-haired 'basin-cut' hairstyle and olive Mediterranean-tone skin. My skinny physical appearance though, masked a very strong and determined mind-set, including a win-at-all-costs mentality on the football pitch; completely camouflaged by my natural pleasant, polite and totally humble attitude – it was if my world was black & white.

> ## WOW
>
> Have you ever considered how certain experiences in your life may have contributed towards you adopting a polarised black & white way of being or thinking?

Both my parents were alcohol dependant and portrayed dark features, each having jet-black hair.

My mother Marlene – whom I affectionally called Ma – held a softness yet sadness about her face, with tranquil green eyes and a 60's-style beehive hairstyle. She had an immensely strong work ethic – as a cleaner – and felt immense pride in being able to 'do her bit'.

Her years of struggle with an uncaring husband had taken its toll. Her forearms bore testimony to this, with razor cuts providing stark evidence of self-harm.

My father Doug also worked very hard as a butcher, before owning a couple of his own shops. He had deep-set penetrative eyes – the sort that delivered a strong disapproving glare to anyone that chose to upset him; his skewed nose the product of his passion for boxing.

He stammered quite badly, something that miraculously disappeared though once he started to deliver a rendition of 'Cry' by Johnnie Ray – usually in some smoke-filled bar, surrounded by his boozing mates.

Although a very hard worker, Doug was a smoker – his nicotine-tinted fingers offering ample proof – as well as being a heavy drinker. He was always very quick to use his fists when dealing with his constantly belittled wife – usually when he'd come home from the pub, worse for wear.

My parents had split up in 1963 when I was just three. After the break-up, Ma and me lived with my matriarchal grandma, Winnie – simply known as Win – on Leybourne Drive, Bestwood.

The multitude of four-block houses on this 1940's-built council estate offered little inspiration by their appearance – basic and grey. The tightly-knit spirit of the community that resided there though, reflected a more colourful and vibrant existence.

Win was a red-head, with an easy-going approach, but one that soon became starkly polarised if crossed. She proudly acknowledged this as part of her west coast of Ireland heritage.

Her portly figure the result of a lifetime's drinking of stout ale, also probably significantly contributed to by a diet of bread and lard.

'Want a cuppa, Paul?' Win enquired of me.

'Yup' was my simple response.

'Why have I only got half a cup?' I curiously asked.

'Cos you leave half anyway,' was my doting grandma's response.

Win's cups of tea had always been a constant source of amusement to me. No matter how many times I asked the same question, I always got the same response from the wily old matriarch.

As a result of my parent's parting, I was supposed to spend a few hours with Doug, every Thursday afternoon – from 2 until 6 – but what a waste of time that was.

'What you want to do s'afternoon son?' Doug would slurringly enquire.

'Let's go to the park and play football,' would always be my response, but to no avail.

The pattern was ever-predictable. On the occasions Doug could even be bothered to turn up, he would do so in an embarrassing drunken state, mumbling away to himself like some delinquent half-wit.

We would end up back at his house, only for him to spend a couple of hours in bed, sleeping off his dinner-time skin-full of booze, before he would then drop me back off home in time for his evening top-up session.

I wasn't bothered though; I had my Ma and Win. I didn't need Doug. Although being extremely poor and not even able to benefit from hand-me-downs as an only child, my home life was blissfully happy.

While very happy, I became acutely aware around the tender age of seven there would only ever be two ways to escape this impoverished, hard-lived existence – sport or education; with the latter not being a realistic contender.

Although a very gifted scholar, I was so passionately in love with Nottingham Forest I was totally blinkered by my emotions. Besides, life on Bestwood was all about hard-nosed practical survival, not sitting behind some desk writing about things.

Apart from being football crazy – believing one day I would wear with pride the red & white of Forest – I had two other fervent passions in my life; music and my black, scampy mongrel dog Rocky.

These were my certainties in life; they provided deep-rooted reassuring comfort – along with the love I got from Ma and Win – and sustained me against the harsh realities of what was unfolding in the outside world.

Although dark, black challenges may present themselves as we travel on our journeys, the one thing that will provide white, radiant light along our paths, is love.

As much as I had enjoyed nearly eight years of my early life in a secure, loving family environment, August 1968 became a time when things were about to dramatically change for me – and not for the better. This was the year that my mother married a man that had lived next door to us.

The first change influenced by the new union, was to uproot from my beloved Bestwood and move out to the rural Nottinghamshire countryside, to a caravan park in Gamston.

I spent the early part of my new life retching daily, due to herds of cattle being shepherded along Bassingfield Lane and leaving their smelly deposits behind *en masse*.

For a city boy like me, it was all very confusing and the start of a far bigger ensuing nightmare – not least because of the behaviour of Mark, my new step-dad. From the outset I sensed instinctively that he disliked me – and I wasn't wrong!

He was a self-employed car cleaner; tall and thin, with a very strong physical presence. His black Brylcreem-laden hair created a modicum of smoothness to the onlooker's eye – contrasted though by the hardness of his face and his constant angry demeanour.

Almost overnight, my emotions had become fragile and vulnerable; I felt so confused and insecure and Ma would constantly try to reassure me that everything would be alright, even though I knew deep down it wouldn't be.

I constantly cried like a baby away from its mother because in effect that's what I was; my whole world had been turned upside down. Everything I had ever known and loved had been taken away from me – Win's love, school and perhaps most of all, the kids from Bestwood with whom I had grown up.

The desperate situation seemed to deteriorate rapidly; each subsequent day compounding the misery from the one before.

'WHAT YOU DOIN' TWAT?' Mark fiercely and unjustifiably demanded, as I innocently sat alone on the grass at the back of the caravan before nervously responding 'just whistling'. 'WELL FUCKIN' DON'T!' was Mark's hurtful retort.

This was the first time I experienced the horrific, practical impact of my new step-dad's vitriolic behaviour and becoming subjected to his stern and aggressive manner.

His nastiness wasn't confined to me though; it was also being vented on Ma.

'FUCKIN' BITCH' was the aggressor's response when Ma dropped a piece of cutlery on the caravan's wooden floor, the ensuing clatter piercing the solitude of Mark humming to himself; it was if he existed in his own crazy bubble.

'You don't like Ma and me, do you?' I nervously and timidly asked him.

'Shut the fuck up and don't ever speak to me like that again, you little bastard!'

His aggressive, crass response rocked me to the core.

At that moment, Ma entered the room and caringly asked 'why's my son crying?'

BANG!

He drew back his right hand and delivered a brutal slap to my concerned mother's face. I looked on helplessly and felt a tightening in my stomach and an instinct – being only being nine years old – to protect my vulnerable mother.

She struggled to hold back the tears, as she gently rubbed her left cheek, to eliminate the pain from this sickening attack.

Irrespective of my obvious fear, I was somehow fuelled by the courage I had learnt from my hardy up-bringing on the streets of Bestwood. Practically though, it was futile; he was too crazed and intimidating and continued with torrents of verbal abuse at the pair of us.

This left me feeling even more confused and very angry; in my mind, I likened him to a wild beast and could no longer think of my new step-dad in any other thoughts or names, than 'The Beast'.

Even that title didn't seem strong enough for him. What was happening to me? Why was I thinking this way? Who was I becoming? All these thoughts started to dominate my ever-changing mind.

I suppose this was the first time in my life that I had experienced such hatred. This piece of shit was vile – evil – and I already detested every single thing about him.

His pitiful attempts at subsequent apologies cut no ice with me. His constant reassurances that it would never happen again disgusted me even more.

I'd often heard stories about Doug's violent behaviour towards Ma and it now seemed that history was repeating itself – but this time with interest on top.

It appeared that as every day went by, I felt more and more hopeless and desperate. It wasn't just this new life and behaviour from The Beast that disturbed me.

I felt like I had been emotionally raped – violated – because I was no longer allowed to listen to my favourite music or enjoy play time with my faithful mongrel Rocky as the dog had been left at Win's.

My new country-boy acquaintances didn't like football either and arguments between Ma and The Beast became ever more frequent – my world felt like it was caving in on top of me.

Because of this, I found myself always nervously awaiting the next physical attack from The Beast and usually I didn't have to wait long before it arrived.

Tensions were consistently building and on a rainy night in late-October, the appalling and barbaric sequel arrived, leaving me feeling so terrified and completely defenceless – like a gazelle ready to be pounced upon by a blood-thirsty lion – that I felt physically sick.

The Beast once again showed his true colours by viciously slapping Ma – three times on this occasion – before turning to me and coldly dictating

'Go to your room, you little bastard!'

'Don't bother son, we're off!' Ma asserted.

Once again, my doting mother defended me – her fragile little boy – by strongly reacting to The Beast.

My mind was awash with conflicting emotions. On the one hand, I wanted to gain revenge on The Beast; on the other, I felt a massive sense of relief – knowing me and my loving mother would be returning home to Bestwood, to Win's, Rocky, to play football and enjoy music again. But most of all, we'd be safe.

Settling back into domestic bliss, Win's trademark tea offer melted me in such a warm and reassuring way.

'Want a cuppa, Paul?' Win asked in her usual caring-like way.

'Yup,' my simple response.

'Why have I only got half a cup?' I curiously asked.

'Cos you leave half anyway,' was my doting grandma's response.

The dialogue between us was ever-predicable – representing my first tentative steps to restoring some certainty into a world that had become very uncertain.

In September 1970, I returned to my old Junior School – Henry Whipple – passing my 11+ exam and gaining a place at the nearby all-boys' High Pavement Grammar School.

Even the harsh reality of England's unsuccessful defence of the World Cup they had won four years earlier could not challenge my sheer elation and happiness. I was home now and able to resume life and my football 'career'.

WOW

We all need something to believe in – a sense of purpose – that fires us so passionately, it gives us a reason to live and continue to make progress.

However, this elation turned out to be short-lived on several accounts. Firstly, I had begun to feel insecure and really down because of the treatment that both me and Ma had suffered from The Beast.

This had scarred me emotionally and little did I know at the time, but this was to have a significant negative knock-on effect in the years to come. Also, football was banned from my new school – only rugby was allowed.

If these two aspects were to cause me distress, this was nothing compared to what transpired later. Within a few weeks, I had to endure the horrific consequences of Ma being re-united with The Beast and once again, my world was shattered.

All his previous promises of change and happiness soon disappeared and the violence and torture returned with a vengeance – and all this when I was still barely eleven years old.

The only solace was that the mobile home in Gamston had been sold and The Beast had acquired a house in Basford, Nottingham.

It may have been a different place, but his old habits soon returned and became even more sickening. He constantly taunted me about my 'crappy football team' and – for no reason at all – often made me stand on one leg, whilst smiling up to the ceiling and saluting the sky.

BANG!

As soon as I flinched, The Beast always delivered at least one thundering slap to my soft, sensitive face, invariably leaving a reddened reminder of his bullying and cowardly acts.

My sole salvation through this living hell was the passionate belief that one day, I would be playing for my beloved football club, Nottingham Forest; but this obsession was now being challenged by a new-found coping mechanism – the demon drink.

Ma had been a secret drinker and by the time I was twelve, I too was regularly helping myself to tots from her stashes of sherry & whisky and soon became addicted.

'What you doin' son?,' Ma sensitively asked me, as I rustled around at the back of the cupboard under the kitchen sink; a rare moment of mother and son bonding time presenting itself while The Beast had popped out.

Her half-hearted question seemed futile because she already knew the answer; this was where the bottles were secretly kept.

'I'm doing what you do Ma,' was my equally unconvincing response.

'Don't son, please – it's a question of bottle and you've got the right one; you don't need drink, it'll kill you'.

Little did I realise at the time, the significance – and the reality - of those words of wisdom from Ma.

We were both petrified and were dealing with our demons within the confines of our own awareness at the time.

I would cringe as I slowly unscrewed the top to the whisky bottle; knowing its repulsive smell would only be unpleasantly surpassed by its disgusting taste. I needed to numb my pain though and this was the only 'medicine' I had come to know.

The sherry wasn't quite as bad, although the immediate warm, fuzzy result of downing a couple of tots, was soon replaced with a longer-lasting taste of stale alcohol and a feeling sick effect.

I was at breaking point and all my ever-growing instincts for survival were severely being tested to the limit.

By now, the abuse, cruelty, neglect and violence experienced at the hands of The Beast were beginning to have a violent knock-on effect to me – compounded even further by witnessing Ma regularly taking beatings.

My world had become very black and I just didn't know what to do anymore – I felt emotionally crippled, violated and full of despair.

> ## WOW
>
> How do we cope with life's traumas? It's a question of bottle. And I chose the one full of the demon drink.

By way of a modicum of salvation though, Forest had really set my heart alight in the 1973-74 season, progressing to the quarter-finals of the prestigious FA Cup in England and drawn away against the mighty Newcastle United Football Club.

At weekend's I wasn't allowed to come down from my bedroom for tea; Ma used to bring me a couple of jam sandwiches and a small piece of malt loaf up on a plate.

Being confined to my bedroom all day, I had no way of knowing what the score was. I had to rely on Ma popping out to the shops at half and full-time; her getting updates from a local shopkeeper that would follow football on his telly, every Saturday afternoon.

The big day arrived on Saturday March 9th 1974...

> ## WOW
>
> In times of distress, we often seek 'crutches'. As well as the demon drink, Nottingham Forest became a powerful emotional crutch for me. I searched externally – but I now know the answer will always be found within.

'I'm so sorry son,' Ma apologetically and tenderly said to me, continuing 'They lost 4-3'.

She delivered the crushing news, like a would-be slayer committing the final, all-decisive blow.

I was speechless – gutted!

At school the following Monday morning, all the boys were talking about the events of that fateful game. It transpired Forest were winning 3-1 at one stage until a pitch invasion by thousands of frustrated Newcastle supporters contributed to the hosts running out 4-3 winners.

However, such were the subsequent protests from Forest, a replay was ordered. On Tuesday 19th March 1974, stalemate resulted from the first game at Everton's Goodison Park ground.

The second replay – two days later – saw the black & white of Newcastle emerge a victorious 1-0 and proceed to the semi-finals.

Such was my total and unswerving emotional attachment to Forest that I had literally lost the will to live. How my beloved team could do this to me, was the question that constantly swirled around in my distorted mind.

Didn't they love me the way I loved them – with every breath in my body? Between The Beast and Forest, all the beautiful memories from my first seven years of life with Ma and Win were being brutally eroded away.

Two days after this excruciatingly painful devastation, my 'betraying' Forest had the chance to restore some of my faith; they were playing away at Fulham's Craven Cottage ground.

However this wasn't meant to be either – they suffered a 2-0 defeat, yet again to a team that played in black & white.

The Beast constantly revelled in my demise and emotional torture, constantly reinforcing a line I'd heard from him many times...

'I've told you before, get that fucking football crap out of your stupid head'.

I literally couldn't take any more and so on Saturday 23rd March, barely two hours after the Fulham defeat – aged just thirteen and a half – I decided to end it all.

The demon drink was no longer strong enough to sufficiently numb the effects of my mental and emotional pain.

Enough was enough!

In my helpless turmoil – aided significantly by a couple of tots of whiskey – I crazily plotted what I would do, to finally end the misery.

Once I could escape from the imprisonment of constantly being confined to my bedroom, there was a secluded area adjacent to Bulwell Common – known as Dicky-Diedows – that I would go to.

On that fateful Saturday, I knew my world was about to change – but certainly not in the way I had anticipated. Around 7pm that evening, I got my usual order to go to the shops for The Beast.

Before I came down stairs, I entered the bathroom and acquired a razor blade and placed it inside my underpants, before putting on shorts, T-shirt and plimsolls and heading to the shops – knowing I would not be returning.

I proceeded onto Dicky-Diedows, sobbing continuously as I relived every callous, cruel and sickening act from The Beast; compounded by the betrayal from my beloved Forest.

The tune of Elvis's *In The Ghetto* constantly whirled in my semi-pickled and tortured mind.

After reflecting on these heart-wrenching experiences, I held my left wrist upwards, with the gleaming razor blade in my right hand – ready to end this nightmare on earth, with one simple swipe.

> ## WOW
>
> Most people experience pivotal moments when life swings from feeling empowered to the other extreme of feeling like a victim – or vice-versa – this turned out to be one of those life-defining moments for me.

After what seemed like an eternity, I experienced an inner warmth. And in a split second, I just intuitively knew this wasn't the answer, as I muttered to myself 'why should I give in because of some dirty piece of shit, like him?'

'How will Ma cope if she's left alone with The Beast?' became the all-dominant self-talk in my mind...who's going to protect her?' and 'what about all the other people that are suffering – who's going to fight for them?'

These probing questions seem to galvanise me and I suppose this was the first time that I'd ever become conscious that my life now had some kind of purpose.

My new-found awareness to fight for others was sufficient to inspire me to drop the blade.

Not that I had the emotional or intellectual intelligence to rationalise it at the time, but it was one of those 'fight-or-flight' moments and I made a decision to never fly again. I somehow had the belief that there was a reason for this test.

If I was experiencing this heartache, surely others would be too? Armed with this insightful breakthrough, I was ready to take on the world and fight anyone that tried to stop me!

With a new-found focus and purpose, I started to become very single-minded and aggressive in my behaviour.

Because of the weight of the responsibility to fight for others, I learnt to create a diversionary tactic – so outsiders wouldn't be allowed to get close to me.

In my distorted mind, closeness equated to pain and suffering and there was no way anyone was going to get close enough. I deliberately started to build a protective shield around me.

Part of this shield included developing another character – one that would allow me to escape and become somebody else; a facade that was perceived by others to be a no-nonsense hard-nut who didn't care about anyone or anything.

My whole mindset had completely changed; it was if a switch had been activated and the light had been turned off, with a new, darker life unfolding; one that now necessitated I create a world that I controlled and I would be significant in.

WOW

Amid the chaos and uncertainty that life can sometimes offer, we all need certainty. In my case, I realised I was meeting this need in a negative, counter-productive way.

'FUCK OFF BASTARD!' was my confrontational reaction to a sixth-form prefect that had a propensity to use his hockey stick on lads that where below him in the school's pecking order, including me.

I continued...'You're an arsehole and I don't give a fuck about you, your mates or this pompous stuck-up school – now piss off!'

WACK!

I felt the full force of hockey stick against my tender backside, before I steadied myself and smacked him – as hard as I could – in the face.

The school playground was suddenly an excited cauldron of violent activity – like a Roman Colosseum – fuelled by the exuberant chants of my peers to 'do him'.

I deliberately rebelled against anything and everything, sabotaging things whenever life began to resemble 'normality'. As I began to embrace this new identity, I started to revel as a rebel with a cause.

This was particularly prevalent at school – on the very few occasions I actually attended – and it was ironically a very amusing incident there that was to begin to close this first eventful chapter of my life.

The Deputy Head – Mr. Watson – came into the last lesson of the day, with about five minutes to go. He asserted to Mr. Jones the RE teacher, 'I've come to collect that boy for detention sir, for fighting with a sixth-form prefect,' as he pointed at me.

Jones duly enquired 'Tommy Jackson, when are you going to learn to behave?'

Watson's face was one of utter amazement as he quizzingly looked at Jones for addressing me as Tommy Jackson.

Tommy Jackson was an Irish international footballer that played for Forest in the 70's and I just took it upon myself to assume this alias at school; with this 'joke' prevailing for nearly three years before my cover was broken.

My peers' initial sniggers couldn't be contained – the whole class burst into belly-aching raptures of laughter. I was unceremoniously marched to the Head's office and duly received extra corporal punishment – six of the best from the cane and similar via the strap.

This was nothing compared to the anticipation of what awaited me once I got home. Because of my new-found commitment to never back down and always fight, I began trembling with anticipation as I sprinted home from school, with all the adrenaline and nervous energy of that hunted gazelle I felt I'd become.

But this time I felt different somehow – I knew I would confront The Beast – the hunted had now become the hunter!

The usual pattern was that I always had precisely ten minutes from 3pm, to sprint from school to home, followed by a cold strip-wash, jam sandwich for tea and then confined to my bedroom until the next morning; other than going to the off-licence for The Beast.

Any deviation from that rigid routine by me always resulted in violence – towards both Ma and me.

After serving one hour's detention, I arrived home at ten past four, only to be met with The Beast's sarcastic and vitriolic question:

'WHERE THE FUCK YOU BEEN. YOU WASTE OF SPACE?'

Previously, I had always been mindful of trying to placate, rather than antagonise him – if only for the sake of Ma – but not this time.

My provocative response was equally assertive as it was cold and spine-chilling.

'I've come to KILL YOU, you sick, twisted bastard!' I growled at him. The Beast instantly launched a sickening and simultaneous physical and verbal attack on me as I became over-powered. But I just wouldn't give in.

I kept taunting him, whilst wiping the streams of crimson blood from my face. As I did so, I glimpsed a bread knife on the table and instinctively lunged to grab it, with only one thought in mind – and it wasn't to cut bread!

I stared into his eyes for what seemed like an eternity, broken only by Ma returning from the shops. I was ready to deliver revenge for all those years of physical, mental and emotional abuse imposed on me and my beloved mother.

'Don't son, please – he's not worth it'.

> ## WOW
>
> Everything starts from awareness. I may have been aware of Ma's plea on a superficial level, but certainly didn't understand what she was actually saying – experience helps us to comprehend things more deeply.

My mother's impassioned plea melted me, but this was no time for me to show weakness – after all, I'd learnt that big boys don't cry.

I just knew by the look in The Beast's eyes that the tide had turned. Just the slight hesitations I picked up from his body language were enough to convince me my fear from him was now over – and he knew it.

The anticipated violent bloodbath didn't materialise. Ma and me simply packed our bags, went back to Win's and left the pathetic, cowardly Beast to a lifetime of bitterness and loneliness.

'I will return and KILL YOU one day – that's a promise!'

I quietly muttered to him – out of Ma's ear-shot – as I went out the door for the last time.

As Ma and me we walked the couple of miles to Win's we talked about what had emerged over the last six years and how we could both start all over again without him.

This proved to be a massive turning point in my life, because I was now free to keep learning about life, loving others and continue my fight to make life better for people that needed help.

Whilst well aware that my own life was full of challenges – particularly from the past – I just knew that I had to soldier on; the world needed me.

By the time I had just passed my 14th birthday – despite all the testing challenges I'd had to tackle and overcome – a whole new world was about to open up to me and I cautiously started to feel hopeful about things, once again.

With my new-found freedom, the winds of change were blowing and this was the first time that I became aware of being able to take back control of my own life, from the jaws of adversity.

I had already successfully overcome so many challenges – or so I thought – and learnt so much along the way, but was now hungry for even more learning and wanted to be someone of significance – someone of influence.

No matter what life throws at you - keep going! There is always success to be found for those that persevere.

PaulLowe**HEARTS**

PART TWO:

THE
BLACK & WHITE
YEARS

I was now on a mission and nothing – or no one – was going to stop me.

The nightmares of watching my dear mother being subjected to sickening abuse and violence – along with my own devastating experiences – gave me a real sense of purpose.

I now saw it as my responsibility to make sure other people didn't suffer in life, embracing my new identity as a perceived no-nonsense hard-nut – this provided me with a sense of certainty, in a world that had become very uncertain.

Still coming to terms with the disappointment of Forest's two 'life-threatening' results to Newcastle and Fulham – the black & white enemies – my new priority was to pursue an unquenchable passion to play for my beloved football team.

As well as The Beast, there remained other 'unfinished business' because I'd never actually seen Forest play. My emotional attachment to them was beyond comprehension, even to the vast majority of my football-crazy peers.

'When you goin' to see Forest play then son?' Ma enthusiastically asked.

'Dunno Ma, need to get some money first,' I happily replied.

'Here, here's a quid,' chipped in Win, continuing 'you deserve it'.

I overwhelmingly appreciated the magnanimous gesture from the ageing matriarch, but this is me, self-reinforcing my deep-seated belief that I don't take things from people – I only give.

Times were very difficult financially for the newly-reunited trio of me, Ma and Win, so I got a job at the local newsagents, doing several newspaper rounds to help make ends meet.

After all, no self-respecting 'Trent Ender' (the Trent End was one of the popular stands at Forest's City Ground) could be seen on the terraces without a cropped haircut, Levi clothing and red Doc Marten boots. 'Dockers' were expensive items at the time, so I devised a cunning plan to get a pair.

One of the Irish lads I used to knock around with – Patrick Nee – had a pair, so I suggested we had a fight and if Patrick won, he'd get a pound. If I won, I'd get the boots.

This plan though, was flawed on two levels – Patrick was a lot bigger and older than me and secondly, the boots were three sizes larger than I needed.

'You set?' Patrick enquired in a gentleman-like, manner, as if we were bound by the Marquis of Queensbury rules.

I didn't respond, simply stared right through him as if he wasn't there, before all hell broke loose in a matter of seconds.

I just switched-off and went for him like a man possessed; my violent conditioning from The Beast meant that I had become oblivious to any of Patrick's blows.

After what seemed like an eternity, he declared...
'STOP – I've had enough!' as we both wiped the crimson evidence from our battle-scarred faces.

I had now got my first bit of Forest 'kit'.

As Patrick handed over the boots, he smugly announced in a soft Irish lilt... 'Here, have 'em – they've got big holes in each sole anyway'.

'No problem!' I smugly retorted, not wanting to lose face, before delivering another couple of jabs to his already bloodied nose.

'That's for takin' the piss' I concluded.

I proudly raced home and promptly cut up an old plastic football to use as insoles. This was fine whilst I stood still but as soon as I began to walk, a large orange circle appeared on the sole of each boot – I didn't care though.

The next piece of my Forest uniform was a Levi denim jacket. This was obtained from a man called Tommy Bohan; a strapping six-foot ex-Teddy Boy from the rough & ready days of 1950's St. Anns in Nottingham.

Tommy knew of my focus and allowed me to take the jacket, so long as I promised to pay him a couple of quid from my paper round money.

To say the jacket was too big would be like saying you might get a little wet if you jumped in the sea! But once again, I was undeterred. I proceeded to cut off the sleeves and attach any relevant Forest sticker or badge I could lay my hands on.

I thought it looked brilliant; it must have – people were constantly staring at me! I couldn't have cared less though; slowly but surely, I was building up my street cred.

I continued to keep absorbing everything I could about my beloved Forest – I read every newspaper match report, listened to all the radio coverage and immersed myself in every possible conversation relating to them.

By the time I had done all this for a month, my long, eagerly-awaited Forest 'debut' to my first match took place; I was 14 when Forest hosted Blackpool just before Christmas 1974.

I spent the whole morning putting on my Dockers (complete with orange holes), Levi jacket (with lots of room to spare) and what seemed like a thousand football scarves.

'How do I look?' I asked, proudly seeking approval from Ma and Win.

No response.

I thought – as I admiringly glanced in the mirror – that I looked astoundingly cool. The reality however, is that I probably looked more like a walking Christmas tree!

Delivering all those heavy newspapers throughout the previous weeks now made sense and it all seemed worthwhile.

The match itself was a lack-lustre 0-0 affair; but I could not have cared less; I wasn't interested in the result.

My emancipation had finally begun and I couldn't wait for Monday morning, to tell all my mates about every scything tackle in defence, every dynamic pass from midfield and every block-busting shot on goal.

My die-hard Forest peers were amazed at my over-zealous enthusiasm for such a boring stalemate, to the point where it was suggested I'd never actually been to a match before!

Undeterred, I eagerly anticipated the next home game a week later against another black & white enemy – local rivals Notts County. Life was now getting better for me and this would continue once Forest had hammered the Magpies – right?

Wrong! Heartbreak appeared yet again – Forest lost and the manager was sacked. What a significant milestone this turned out to be though, both for me and Forest.

Within a matter of days, the football club appointed the hugely outspoken Brian Clough as the new manager. In spite of this heart-wrenching defeat to our adversaries, it presented me with a chance to be influenced by a strong male role model.

Previously, my only male influences had come from Doug and The Beast and I hopefully searched for that positive father-figure; someone to look up to and be inspired by.

I instantly warmed and resonated with Brian's perceived brash, arrogant persona and certainly appreciated the improvement he was making at Forest. Emotionally, I felt as if I was becoming re-energised. I was committed – more than ever – to wearing that Garibaldi Red shirt. I began practising my football skills morning, noon and night.

A school mate (Andy Green) and I wrote to Forest asking for a trial and the club offered us both that opportunity. However, Andy's excitement was cut short, due to him having his ankle broken in training – by me!

During a practise match, us two would-be footballers went in for a 50/50 ball and as someone that was used to going in hard with far lesser odds of winning – both in football and life – I relished these 'equal opportunities' and tackled opponents knowing there would only ever be one winner.

CRACK!

Andy's left ankle snapped like a walnut being hit with a hammer. I offered no emotion to my beleaguered opponent; I simply walked away as all the other lads rallied around him.

In the spring of 1975, I went to the trial at the club alone and beamed with pride as I stepped out on the hallowed City Ground turf.

As it turned out, I wasn't good enough to make it as a professional footballer; my Forest career was over before it had even started. This time though I wasn't devastated – just the opposite.

The confidence I gained from massively being dragged out of my comfort zone and taking on an immense challenge like this, was immeasurable. Deep down, I knew I wasn't good enough – I just needed something to believe in.

My belief in Forest though, was sorely being tested. One of the early games of the new 75-76 season resulted in the black & white curse striking again.

Forest was playing rivals Notts County and at parity with one minute to go, Les 'Bomber' Bradd scored for the Magpies. I was inconsolable and felt physically sick for days on end.

The gut-wrenching feelings I experienced matching those I'd had when I first witnessed The Beast's cowardly and depraved behaviour towards Ma.

As with the two games against other black & white opposition – Newcastle and Fulham – in March 1974, I couldn't comprehend this betrayal from a team I devotedly loved.

WOW

Betrayal – what betrayal? My insecurity and vulnerability meant I constantly wanted to control things that were out of my control.

Isn't the truth that we need to focus only on the things that are within our own control?

My emotional attachment was served well over the ensuing five years though. Forest gained promotion, as well as winning a multitude of domestic and European honours.

However, during this time-span – just as I had felt inexcusably let down by my club losing to black & white teams – I wasn't being completely faithful to my adored team either; girls started to compete for my emotions and the females seemed to be winning hands-down!

'Can you tell me where Leybourne Drive is please?' A plumpish forty-something woman politely asked as she turned around from her seat in front of me, on the number 28 bus; accompanied by a Lee Van Cleefe look-alike and a sandy-coloured Collie dog.

'Sure, what number?' I curiously responded.

My interest heightened dramatically as the dark-haired lady revealed the house number, resulting in me exclaiming 'that's next door to me'.

This was the first time – in spring 1975 – that I met Eileen and her husband Ron, along with Sheba, their beautiful canine. Within a couple of weeks, the new neighbours had moved in and I immediately seemed to click with Eileen.

'Ron's a real bastard, you know – never trust him,' Eileen confidentially shared with me as we got to know each other.

'Why you with him then?' I bluntly replied.

'Agoraphobia, I've got agoraphobia and I need him to help me,' she submissively conceded.

Although old enough to be my mother, we really understood each other and enjoyed a great connection. Maybe this was due to the fact she too had a life full of struggles and challenges – particularly with Ron, her husband for ten years?

Although our relationship wasn't sexual, there was a closeness and an intimacy between us – we trusted each other implicitly. Part of Eileen's trust in me, was to confide the abuse she had suffered at the hands of her husband; he was a violent alcoholic. Upon first hearing this, all my protective – yet defensive – mechanisms kicked in.

Déjà vu – yet again!

Within a matter of three months, her errant husband had moved out, leaving the legacy of a black eye for the abused and insecure female. This made my blood boil and I felt huge torrents of fierce and uncontrollable rage and anger.

'I'll kill the bastard if ever I see him again,' I reassuringly promised her.

'Paul, don't – please,' she pleaded, terrified, continuing 'all my life I've experienced violence and abuse and it doesn't get anyone anywhere'.

Her opening three words sounding all too familiar and reminding me – verbatim – of what Ma had said to me as I confronted The Beast the previous year.

As we continued to build our trusting relationship, I reciprocated the many leaps of faith that Eileen had taken with me, by sharing that I really like the young woman that lived the other side of her – Donna.

As the months went by, Eileen got to know her other neighbours, particularly the object of my affection, Donna.

Ironic that I wanted to get together with someone I had known virtually all my life – Donna had lived on Bestwood as long as me – by the match-making of a relative stranger.

'What if she rejects me?' I shared my concern about rejection, with Eileen.

'Don't worry, just be yourself,' was my new confidante's reassuring reply.

In the summer of 1976 – when I was barely sixteen – Donna and I got together and within a few weeks, we moved in together as lodgers – with Eileen.

Donna was a diminutive, cautious type of girl and despite being three years older than me, she lacked confidence and her whole demeanour was akin to the safe and certain 'girl next door' mould.

In my erratic, unstable world though, this was okay – I craved certainty after all the previous turbulence that had evolved.

The reality was though, that Donna also wanted certainty and stability in her life and she couldn't cope with my volatile personality and drinking binges.

Despite my constant reassurances that I would look after her, I think she instinctively knew I would assume the role of a caring brother, rather than that of a sensitive, loving partner, reinforced by her assertion:

'We can't be together Paul – you're wild and a rule unto yourself,' she continued with her soul-destroying verdict…'I need someone that will take care of me, not someone that threatens to kill anyone that upsets me'.

Her parting words delivered the final blow…'You upset me, you're going to kill yourself – you already are'.

I didn't understand her profound words; conning myself that she was the one with the problem, not me.

The relationship was doomed and we both moved back to our respective homes, either side of Eileen.

WOW

Until we detach ourselves from criticizing and blaming others, we will never move forward. We need to take responsibility for our own beliefs, thoughts, words, actions and results.

Shortly after we had gone, Eileen's husband returned to her and for a while, they seemed to enjoy domestic bliss. Remembering her warning, I began to watch him like an eagled-eyed bird of prey, waiting to pounce.

The friction between me and him became intolerable and Eileen heartbreakingly requested I didn't pop round and see her anymore; giving the newly-reunited couple a chance to build bridges.

The devastation I felt was immeasurable and I tried to convince her that no good would come of it; he was bad news and I should know, I'd had enough experience of shit in my life, even though I was still very young.

Shockingly within a matter of months of Eileen getting back with her ex, he had murdered her.

I had returned home to Win's in the early hours of a Sunday morning after a 'Palais Special' – a one-night stand – to witness flashing blue lights everywhere.

Neighbours were on the streets gossiping and already drawing their own judgemental conclusions as to what had happened and why. The pleasures of the previous few hours were wiped out in a flash.

I was devastated. The earth had move beneath my feet and my balance was lost.

My mind was awash with conflicting emotions; if only I hadn't walked away from her, she'd still be alive. Yet again, I was totally consumed by anger and guilt, believing that if I had been there I would have been able to protect her.

All this had a very profound effect upon me and all of a sudden, Forest winning a few games of football seemed so meaningless.

I was so hurt and confused and despite my rough Jack-the-lad image, I felt an emotional pain so deep and excruciating; way beyond any physical pain I'd ever endured in the past.

As much as I had developed a hard exterior to males, this mask easily slipped where females were concerned. I trusted the security of knowing how protective and loving they could be – Ma and Win had ensured that – so I was never afraid to show my emotional, vulnerable and sensitive side to womenfolk.

Even though my first testing experience with Donna, I intuitively knew that love was the answer to my life's confusion and pain.

'Why does life have to be so complicated?' I painfully asked Ma, following up with a far more pertinent question...'and why have you gone back to The Beast, he's evil?' These questions the result of her reunion with him some weeks previously.

'I've made my bed son, so I must lie on it,' my doting mother gently responded.

This metaphoric explanation was beyond my comprehension. For me, it was very simple - The Beast was depraved and that was it – it was black or white.

> **WOW**
>
> Interesting how we can become prisoners in our own minds by letting black, destructive thoughts dominate us. With The Beast though, the reality was simple. He represented total darkness – at the time, I could see no white light at all.

Because of my family's west coast of Ireland roots, I found connection through mixing with Irish fraternities; regularly visiting the allotments (caves) of the men-folk on Sunday mornings for a nip or two of Potcheen (home-made Irish potato wine) and tales of bare-knuckle fighting – usually led by Irish Joe from Connemara.

I even started to believe the girl I'd settle down with would be a 'dark-haired Colleen'.

The red hot summer Queen's Jubilee Year of 1977 also meant that I started work, initially in a trophy factory as a labourer.

Despite being academically gifted, I had wasted my secondary education at High Pavement Grammar School – constantly rebelling against the Victorian-style discipline and bullying from the prefects. I had been too pre-occupied with survival to be bothered about academia.

My first work experience was bitter-sweet. On the bitter side, most of my new work colleagues were die-hard Forest boys and would go to matches – home and away – usually the worse for drink.

With me having my own drinking binges, this seemed like a hand-in-glove union. The usual modus operandi for away games was to drink a half-bottle of whiskey each on the train, before arriving at the opposition's ground.

The late 70's was rife for football violence and whilst I was more than game for a good old 'tear up' with rival supporters, I constantly felt disgust at some of the sickening violence I witnessed – particularly towards women and kids.

Having been raised against the back-drop of this type of cowardly behaviour, I made a conscious decision to break away and keep to myself.

After leaving the trophy factory, I spent a couple of years as a welder in a local factory. The work was mind-numbingly boring with the only consolation being it paid reasonably well – certainly sufficient to give Win some house-keeping money and have enough to fund my ever-increasing alcohol dependency.

Billy had got me the job and was probably responsible for one of the most humorous things we ever did between us. When I was sixteen, I got a Honda C50 moped. Two thoughts constantly prevailed around this:

Firstly, Billy riding pillion one day – his 6-foot-plus, 17-stone frame ensuring the engine laboured along at a ridiculous 3mph; it would probably have been quicker for us to have walked to work.

Secondly, the number of times I fell off it – being distracted by looking at passing girls – and usually ending up crashing into the back of a car or bus.

Continuing the humour theme, the two of us used to break the hum-drum monotony of working in a dirty, noisy factory by having 'singing' competitions.

'OUT ON THE WINDING WINDY MOORS...' I would challenge the noise of the background industrial machinery with a high-pitch Kate Bush-like impression.

Billy responding with... 'HEATHCLIFFE, IT'S ME – CATHY...'

I couldn't cope with the tedious monotony of working robot-like in one space all day. It reminded me of all the years I'd been confined to my bedroom, under the barbaric control of The Beast.

I needed freedom and variety in life and this wasn't it.

Aware that my life was spiralling out of control and because I felt I needed some real focus, I made an application to join the Royal Marines in early 1980 aged

19 – at the same time I was also offered a job with the GPO as a cable jointer.

I was so confused about my identity, realising the façade I was presenting to the outside world was a massive lie.

Conversely, I also knew that I had immense strength physically and mentally; and I certainly had a deep sense of purpose – to serve and protect.

Although at heart I was a naturally, caring type of person, I was becoming ever-aware that this fitted well with the true warrior inside of me. I was also someone that wanted to fight for others who couldn't fight for themselves; rationalising this as the legacy of my early unjust challenges.

In my mind, the Royal Marines was the answer.

After undergoing several extremely demanding tests, I was offered the chance to join this elite fighting corps – it felt so right for me – and I knew it was time to remove my 'mask'.

Despite my heavy drinking bouts, I would then go on the wagon and commit to hard stints of physically and mentally demanding exercise – this was the epitome of my black & white mind-set.

WOW

As we raise our awareness, we learn that even things like having a black & white mind-set can have its positives.

A couple of years after breaking up with Donna, I started courting a beautiful soul called Lynne; she adored me and despite my alcohol dependency she stuck by me through thick and thin.

Her attractive looks – with blonde hair and piercing blue eyes – accompanied an ever-smiling face, reflecting a well-balanced outlook on life and certainly a robustly stable influence in my extremely erratic world.

She served as a constant uplift to me in my black, negative phases of life; her positive personality reinforcing the inspiring experience.

Because of my underlying issues, I began to feel as if I wasn't worthy of such a gift and harshly sabotaged everything we had together.

'I don't deserve you,' I'd constantly declare to her, not realising that this only served to plant seeds of doubt in her mind. This self-undermining belief began to permeate her trust in me.

The inevitable split-up occurred and the result was I predictably just hit the bottle even harder and harder – the pattern was all too familiar as I continued on my self-destructing, downward spiral.

My all-or-nothing mind-set was great when I was on a dry run and working towards achieving something positive, but totally destructive when I was on a bender.

In effect, I was living a polarised black & white existence, with darkness becoming ever more frequent.

I started to refer to my drinking as the black part of my life; abstinence reflected the white.   Either way, I instinctively knew I had to sort this madness out.

I was missing Lynne like crazy so I had a creative and ingenious plan to get her back; or so I thought at the time.

When I next came off the drink – at the end of my self-imposed stint – I would take the GPO job short-term, get back with Lynne and if I was offered a post with the Royal Marines the two of us would then start a new life in Devon.

As a result of subsequent events, Meatloaf's *Two Out Of Three Ain't Bad* propounded in my tortured mind.

Two out of three – firstly, I did take the GPO job.

Secondly, I didn't manage to get back with Lynne; I had broken her heart and she wasn't going to ever trust me again.

Thirdly, I was offered a place in Lympstone, Devon to start recruit training as a Royal Marine.

Undeterred though, I only viewed this as a temporary setback; I was confident I would win her back and things would soon be back on-track. I decided to temporarily put the Royal Marines on hold, whilst I patched things up with her.

I duly visited the recruiting office and ignorantly informed the officer-in-charge that I would be joining the next cohort of recruits, after I'd got back with my girlfriend.

The stern, disapproving look of the officer was more than an adequate substitute for his silence.

'I'm going to make this work for us, you'll see'.

My words to Lynne were based more on an emotionally plea, rather than a concrete commitment.

'No Paul, you won't – there's no way back,' she gently whispered.

It's amazing how eight simple words could have such a devastating effect on someone's life – my life.

After this bombshell, I believed my only way forward, was to forget about women for the time being and start a new life – as far away from Nottingham I could get – and join the Royal Marines.

After starting with the GPO, the first man I was teamed up with was a former Royal Marine – Jimmy Blackstock. Once me and Jim got talking, the latter wisely advised me...'Join up son, you'll regret it for the rest of your life if you don't'.

Little did I know then, how Jim's wise words would stand the test of time.

I respectfully listened to his sound reasoning and was reassured by the fact that he actually knew the recruiting officer, Alan.

'I know you're right Jim – I need to draw a line under everything that's gone off in my life,' was my simple acceptance.

As a 19-year-old, this felt like everything that had previously happened, was only the foundation for this new, exciting opportunity.

Jim and me promptly proceeded to the recruitment centre with a view to me taking up the previously offered place. After the usual greetings and pleasantries between two old comrades, Jim announced to Alan...

'Paul's here Al – he wants to take up the place you offered him'.

Alan's response was as equally startling to Jim as it was alarming to me.

'I'm surprised at you Jim – you know better than anyone that the Royal Marines are the cream of the crop and you only ever get one chance with us'.

He continued and asserted...'Paul was tailor-made for us – we had a good chat about his life and we both agreed it would have been a great fit. But he asked us to wait for him – we don't wait for anyone – so it's over!'

> ## WOW
>
> **Trust is like a fine porcelain object – it's a beautiful thing to have but will never be the same if you mishandle it and allow it to be shattered.**

Back to square one. This rejection was amplified by Lynne's assertive defiance that the relationship was definitely finished and if I really loved her, I'd leave her alone to pick up the pieces of her life that I'd totally shattered.

This double-rejection knocked me for six and tested – once again – my previously-proven immense durability and tenacity to the extreme and beyond.

Despite my ongoing emotional turmoil, I knew I needed to keep my mind and body strong. The paradox being, both served to sustain me as a hardened drinker whenever I fell off the wagon.

Whatever I did, I needed to be the very best at it – even at drinking, with all its negative and destructive outcomes.

At the beginning of the 80's – with me now in my early twenties – I had changed dramatically from my early days of being a skinny, wiry child.

Although as a man I was average height, my body and especially my legs had become very broad and muscular – due to endless running as a child, trying to keep to The Beast's timescales – significantly conditioned by playing football, rugby and generally being dedicated to hard, physical training.

Through my drunken brawls I had developed a boxer's skewed nose and had become very powerful physically with speed and lightning reflexes emerging as a natural part of my nervous make-up.

In the summer of 1982 – aged 21 – I left Win's house at Bestwood and got a flat. This fitted in perfectly for me because now, I had selfishly absolved myself of any responsibility towards looking after my ailing grandma.

Shortly after – because of her declining health – my passionate, fiery and caring Win was moved into sheltered accommodation, to Pear Tree Court at Basford, Nottingham. The old 3-bedroom home at Bestwood had become unmanageable; especially after her enduring a leg amputation, due to gangrene, as a result of many years' heavy smoking.

By running away, I was free to carry on in my own shallow and distorted way; rapidly ceasing to become the naturally caring, sensitive person deep down I knew myself to be.

I'd now gone from being a potential elite team player in the Royal Marines to a selfish loner – and some would say, a loser.

This awareness started to create consistent guilt feelings in me. I often thought to myself, how could I walk away from someone that had contributed so lovingly to my life?

Against this back-drop of shameful confusion, I began courting Beverley – a girl I had known since childhood – who was very hard working and respectable.

Whilst Bev was very similar to Lynne in her soft, caring and sensitive nature, she was very different appearance-wise. As a dark-haired girl, she was more my 'type'.

I often cogitated how previously, I had become attracted and fell in love with a blonde – as one of my early formative beliefs was that I didn't like blondes.

Bev showed immense loyalty and patience with me as her new boyfriend and continued to invest in our relationship.

This quickly progressed and she began to spend more and more time at my flat.

It was New Year's Day 1983 and as we enthusiastically discussed our plans for the future – particularly our imminent wedding, a few weeks later in April - as the phone rang; suddenly my jovial demeanour was instantaneously replaced by a more serious, worried frown.

'Aren't you going to answer it?' Bev enquired.

I hesitated – intuitively knowing it was going to be bad news. It was!

'FUCKING HELL!'

I screamed as I picked up the TV and threw it through the second floor window of our flat, before turning to the walls and delivering a volley of rapid, powerful punches at them; my knuckles quickly bearing the proof of the ferocity of punches, with a crimson coating of sticky blood.

'Stop it Paul, please,' was the impassioned plea from Bev.

'Fuck off woman – I don't need you or anyone else in my life – JUST FUCK OFF!'

Bev's continued appeals for reasoning fell on deaf ears. I was beyond either consoling or reasoning. At this time, my distraught future wife packed a bag and beat a hasty retreat to the calm sanctuary of her parents.

She didn't need me to confirm the phone call was from Ma, delivering the heart-breaking news that Win had died the night before – aged 76.

As an old-school matriarch, Win was so resilient, strong and as solid and tough as a majestic oak tree.

After her death, I waged war on society. I took it upon myself to be judge, jury, and executioner towards any Tom, Dick, or Harry who I perceived was a bully.

Ever-mindful of my own self-destruct mechanisms, I consciously switched focus and decided to really vent my anger and budding hatred on the outside world instead.

WOW

Interesting how we can subconsciously reflect behaviours. It seemed I was now emulating The Beast by carrying on with the need to control everything in my world.

The predictable pattern of alcohol addiction remained constant though and despite me getting myself into lots of trouble - drunken fights and the like - Bev stuck by me.

Within a year of courting, we married and were soon expecting our first child. This new-found family life provided me with pleasant flashbacks to my formative years as a young boy. But the relationship wasn't without its challenges.

My perception of life was the black got blacker and the white seemed whiter.

Regardless of having a good job, nice flat and a new family, my world wasn't built upon stable foundations. I couldn't erase the memories of The Beast's barbaric behaviour and as much as sheer will-power and determination would temporarily provide respite, the reality was my life had become a roller-coaster.

By now, I had developed a mind-set where I fully expected things to go wrong and call it a self-fulfilling prophecy, but I never seemed to have to wait long.

In the autumn of '83 and born prematurely, our newly-expected boy Thomas arrived – still-born!

As a mother, Bev was grief-stricken; she was beyond comfort. Rather than being man enough to find the strength to support my grieving wife, I immersed myself in my own, pitiful world – cue a massive drinking binge that lasted for weeks on end.

Once again, it seemed like there was an addictive cycle at work – far bigger than the alcoholic one.

One of the things that I was becoming even more aware of though, was the power of love.

As much as all the devastating chaos caused by my black phases of life, it seemed diluted as I clung to the memories of my first seven years and used them as an unshakeable foundation to build up new levels of this all-powerful emotion.

Picking up the pieces again, Bev and me left our flat and purchased a house in nearby Bulwell.

The epitome of our love arrived a year and sixteen days after losing our first child – when a beautiful daughter – Amy Louise made her entrance into the world.

Although struggling to control my emotions for different, more joyous reasons, I went into default mode and 'celebrated,' wetting our new-born's head with one almighty bender again lasting several weeks.

This was the storm before the calm though. Amy's birth seemed to have a massive calming effect on me, to the point where I settled into domestic bliss for a few months and thoroughly enjoyed the rigours of a self-imposed physical training regime.

Five-mile runs every morning as well as supplementing physical activities – such as boxing, football and rugby – became the norm for my life.

Happiness also presented itself, in the form of Ma getting married a year later. She and her third husband – a good man named Cyril – started a new life together in nearby Bestwood Village, an old mining community and it pleased me beyond words to know that she had finally found some well-deserved joy.

Her first husband and my father – Doug – was a wife-beating alcoholic and The Beast was sick and evil beyond description.

But true to form, I was ever-expectant of a black phase to show itself and it duly obliged.

During my many previous episodes, I'd had a couple of petty brushes with the law, without being charged with anything.

The spring of '85 changed all that and at the age of 25 I was convicted of assaulting a work colleague; a whistle-blower who had written a letter to the management – highlighting colleagues' perks done in works time – for his own personal gain.

Being a 'grass' was considered the ultimate treachery in my complicated values system – a by-product of those early years of survival.

Although I wasn't one of those named in the letter, I felt this was betrayal and so took it upon myself to be judge, jury and executioner and punched the Judas that had sent the letter.

For the ensuing twelve months, this created tension with the management and I – the would-be vigilante – was subsequently sacked by the company. To make ends meet, I tried my hand at becoming a taxi driver, but it didn't last, due to the ridiculously long hours and exceptionally poor pay.

No matter – an injection of pure, unbridled love came into our lives on World Cup Final Day 1986, in the form of another beautiful baby girl called Hayley – named after my favourite actress, Hayley Mills.

Yet again, if there was one thing that seemed to dramatically dilute all the horrors of my turbulent past, it was love. My sense of purpose was heightened beyond description and helped guide me towards some light in a world that often seemed pitch-black.

The ensuing two years were mainly ones dominated by unemployment for me. This resulted in us having to sell the family home and be re-housed at the place of Bev's and my childhood – Bestwood Estate.

This became the catalyst though for an unprecedented depth of despair. I was unemployed and despite having no money of my own, I managed to spend most days in the pub; or drinking anything I could get my hands on – just for a 'hit'.

Any self-respect that I'd previously clung to had now gone. I'd go out daily in the same clothes and just let myself go completely.

One bitterly cold February night in my late twenties, I walked home – for about four miles – from an all-day boozing session at a well-known Blues Club.

The heavy snow of the blizzard easily penetrated my T-shirt, shorts and plimsolls – ensuring my skin was permeated by the cold, harsh elements like a sponge immersed in water.

As I reached home, I fumbled and opened the gate, witnessing the snow-clad front garden and collapsed into its enveloping white blanket – lying there like a weak, hopeless soul just waiting to die.

Bev must have heard the noise as I tried to open the gate; she looked out and saw her irresponsible husband in his most vulnerable child-like form.

'I'm calling an ambulance,' she stated as I struggled to hear her words.

'No – don't!' I barely mustered, before reasserting...'Just don't'.

I ended up with double-pneumonia and despite having a multitude of symptoms – shivering, massive sweats (Bev having to change the sheets three times a day), excruciating chest pains and rapidly becoming weaker – I was treated by paramedics but refused to go hospital for the necessary treatment.

My stubbornness almost cost me my life as the weight continued to drop off me at an alarming rate over the ensuing days.

I selfishly wanted to die. My distorted thinking based on all the things I'd done wrong when I was younger; rationalising it must have been me that was at fault for the way The Beast treated me – that was my punishment for being a bad person.

Of course, that was utter crap – and somehow, I knew it.

By now, the white phases were getting even shorter and the black phases longer. Many distorted thoughts and emotions dominated; these in the form of my unfinished business from a seed that had been planted fourteen years previously.

THE BEAST!

WOW

A certain cliché says time's a great healer – it can also be a powerful way to ferment dark, devastating thoughts and destructive actions.

As much as I had tenaciously refused to give in and let my demons completely overpower and destroy me, I had never dealt with the nightmares that evolved from the abusive and violent upbringing at the hands of The Beast. More pertinently, I'd been unable to erase my promise that one day I would return and kill him.

That fateful day came when I was 27; it was the summer of '88 when something just snapped inside of me and I was now ready to exact revenge.

This was made even more apparent by the fact I was now living with Ma and Cyril; I'd left Bev and the kids, because inside, I felt inadequate and underserved of their unconditional love.

I had developed and perfected the art of self-destruction – probably down to years of being undermined and callously taunted by The Beast's consistent assertion:

'You're nothing boy and never will be. No one will ever love you and you'll fuck everything up you ever touch'.

I genuinely believed Bev and our beautiful daughters would be better off without me. They'd got a lovely, secure home and didn't need a drunken brawler like me around.

I'd further convinced myself because I had the reassurance that Bev had a good support network around her – particularly her own loving and loyal family. This reference point had been such a strong and solid foundation from my own earlier years, growing up on Bestwood with Ma and Win.

Twenty tortuous, topsy-turvy years had elapsed since I had first met The Beast and during that hell on earth, I had never managed to come to terms with what had transpired.

I'd learnt to overcome physical pain, but the emotional suffering was something else completely. I'd turned to alcohol as a crutch to survive; the irony being this also pushed me down into deeper and darker depths.

I sat in the local Deerstalker pub in Bestwood and lost count of the number of comments that hazily passed through my ears from the drinkers, about 'looking like a man possessed who was going to kill someone' – I was!

I sat there, recalling every sadistic act, every tortuous humiliation but most of all, the mental and emotional abuse plus physical violence The Beast had inflicted upon Ma and me.

Having left the pub, I set off and walked the couple of miles to meet with fate. Just before midnight, I arrived at The Beast's house, which was all in darkness as I paraded up and down outside the front window like a vigilant Marine.

BANG!

The red mist descended and I kicked in the front door. I knew The Beast slept on the settee and made straight for him.

'Now then YOU FUCKIN' TWISTED FREAK – judgement day has come – I'M GONNA FUCKIN' KILL YOU!,' I hysterically ranted at him.

'Don't – please, don't – I'm so sorry for everything,' he timidly and pathetically reacted.

The pitiful, cowardly pleas were lost on me as my mind automatically went back fourteen years and the moment I'd picked up the bread knife to kill him. History was repeating itself but this time, there would be no mistake.

I gripped my screwdriver tightly, pointing it right at his left eye.

'Which one do you want first, slag?' I demanded and followed up with 'cos that one's for Ma and the other one's for me'.

'AAAAAAAAAAAAAAAAAAAAAAAGH!'

A screaming yell pierced the calm evening silence. In the early hours of the following morning, the police arrived at Ma's house in Bestwood Village and arrested me.

WOW

Isn't life full of ironies? As a result of my intended revenge the one thing I had come to rebel against – authority and control – was about to be enforced on me by the police!

After spending hours and hours in a cell, I struggled to remember anything – as the police attempted to interview me – other than constantly enquiring 'what happened?'

The up-shot was, someone had followed me that night and as I drew back my hand to deliver a fateful blow, the

64

Samaritan had hit me on the back of the head and stopped me from killing The Beast, before he dumped me back at Ma's.

It emerged that The Beast had been reprieved from death, but had phoned the police straight after. Nonetheless, I was charged with threats to kill and remanded in custody for three weeks at HMP Lincoln.

During that time, Ma had bumped into Bev on Bulwell Market a few days later and told my estranged, worried wife about the recent events. Bev's maternal and protective instincts kicked in.

'Please Marlene, just tell him I want him back – we all miss him and the kids need their dad'.

I subsequently got bail and was re-united with Bev. Her and Ma had come to court to present new mitigating background evidence – through my solicitor – and we proceeded to pick up the pieces of our fragmented life together.

Nearly four months later in October 1988, there was a new family addition for Bev and me – the arrival of our baby boy, Dayne. As with his two sisters before him, he brought sheer unadulterated joy into our lives.

I settled into work – as a cable jointer contracting in the south-east of England – earning exceptional money. Working away gave Bev and me some time to think about our life together and what would be best for our three beautiful kids.

Apart from this, one of the things I wanted to find out, was who was responsible for saving two lives? Firstly, my own and not having to serve a life sentence in prison; and secondly that of The Beast – although I couldn't have cared less about him.

Ironic that – just like the police – I made 'extensive enquiries' and wasn't able to establish the identity of the double-saviour. I wasn't surprised though. I existed in a community culture where people just took action, but nobody ever knew anything.

I was determined more than ever, to put all previous pain and suffering behind me.

I wanted to make a fresh start, despite an imminent court trial for the threats to The Beast. At the end of autumn 1988, I received a phone call from my solicitor...

'You're in court tomorrow for your trial – be there,' he solemnly dictated.

I had been warned that the law often works in strange ways and it was possible I could get a five-year sentence for this offence. I wasn't worried though – I knew the very significant mitigation I offered was both genuine and really strong.

I wasn't a mindless violent thug and certainly wasn't a bully. However much I had become confused about my identity, I knew for certain I was a caring, loving warrior at heart.

At the trial, the judge listened intently as the catastrophic sequence of events relating to my life was laid bare to strangers in an open court – I felt violated and extremely angry.

Why should I have to explain myself because of something that occurred as a result of years of appalling behaviour from The Beast? After all, me and Ma never asked for the pain and suffering we had to endure.

We never asked for his sick and depraved actions, resulting in me sometimes catching Ma out with a razor blade in her hand, ready to end her misery, just as I had done in March 1974.

Because I was perceived as turning my life around (again) – combined with the extremely unpleasant history of the case – the potential prison sentence never emerged and whilst I appreciated my freedom, I was not happy with the outcome.

What about the moral injustice of The Beast inflicting years of suffering on two people; yet being able to carry on unpunished, I angrily cogitated.

This was a key breakthrough in my life though – I learnt that love was a far more powerful option than hate. Like everything else in my life back then, I thought about things in black & white terms and there always had to be a winner and a loser – never a compromised 'draw'.

WOW

This was one of my major life epiphanies, which set me on my path of emergence from the forest.

My many and diverse learning experiences were starting to have a really profound effect on me, realising how our decisions can influence our lives.

I had learnt – the hard way – that change can come about if the pain is a strong enough lever. If not, things will simply stay the same or worsen.

Change was certainly something that I was determined to implement, even though at this time, I was still stuck with a black & white polarised belief system.

Since Forest's majestic success in the late 70's-early 80's, I had lost a lot of my football focus. So much had happened since then and – although I still followed their results – I very rarely went to any matches.

But, I was at Hillsborough on that fateful day of April 1989 – for the Forest v Liverpool FA Cup semi-final when 96 Liverpool supporters tragically lost their lives – as well as hundreds receiving injuries in a massive human crush – due to a serious lack of crowd control and effective safety measures being in place.

Such was the effect the horrific event had on me, I wanted to do something to help.

Of course, no amount of money raised would ever compensate for a lost life – let alone 96 – but I empathically felt compelled to organise a sponsored walk from Forest's City Ground to Anfield in Liverpool, to raise money for the Hillsborough Appeal Fund.

Having set about the task – and publicising it on local radio – I subsequently received a letter and £10 donation from a local nun known as Sister Ann.

She promised to see me off from Nottingham, along with another guy Steve, who had kindly agreed to join me on the walk. We were met by the compassionate nun on the May Bank Holiday Saturday morning. Although physically, she appeared as a frail old lady, the power of the reassuring words she gently spoke to the pair of us were never forgotten:

'You will struggle badly on your journey but God will be with you'.

Initially, I didn't give it too much thought, but then on the Bank Holiday Monday – after two and a half days' walking – those words were to become very significant.

By now, I was struggling really badly to walk; my legs were rigidly stiff and my feet were blistered and constantly bleeding. All my reserves of ego-driven stubbornness were being stretched to the absolute limits, but I wouldn't give in.

As I hobbled along, a middle-aged couple pulled up in a car and – seeing my obvious distress – enquired if there was anything they could do to help. I obtusely declined.

A few more miles further along, the same car was there again. This intrigued me because we had walked through a couple of crossroads since and the couple would have had no way of knowing which direction Steve and I would have taken.

The persistent couple offered us both a drink, which we accepted with gratitude. As we took a breather, the husband of the pair unfolded how the previous night he had received a message from God, simply directing him to drive around because someone would need help.

Although Steve was okay, I clearly wasn't. By now, my inability to rationalise the pair's love and compassion was unnerving me.

I felt affronted and privately snarled at Steve... 'How dare they suggest I need help?' I give help to others – you're not allowed to give it to me,' I proudly announced.

However, this stubborn attitude was challenged as Sister Ann's previous potent words came back into my mind. No matter how hard I tried to catch the Good Samaritans out, it became blatantly obvious that neither of them knew the Sister or anyone else connected to Nottingham.

Softened by this intervention and perception, I reluctantly accepted the kind offer of a lift and they drove us four miles to the next destination in Warrington.

After three and a half days of walking and hobbling, we finally reached Liverpool Football Club.

Notwithstanding all my superficial bravado, I found it extremely humbling to be treated with the love and connection from the club's management team; as well as the genuine hospitality from supporters in the nearby Arkle pub.

It wasn't lost on me that this was the second time a Good Samaritan had entered my world and intervened.

This set my mind thinking about the power of faith, I recalled how I used to pray as a kid, so that Ma would stop crying, after being attacked by The Beast; and that she wouldn't try and kill herself because of him.

I also became confused about the many conflicts that I had experienced in the context of religion because people often asked whether I was green (Catholic) or Blue (Protestant).

My answer was as consistently clear as it was blatant and blunt:

'Fuck off and mind your own business,' I further asserted, before continuing…'people are people and no one has the right to judge another; no matter who they are and what they are'.

Part of my early survival lessons taught me that people invariably want to pigeon-hole others and label them.

A lot of people took exception to my single-minded stance. The real cause of subsequent fights wasn't about my religion or faith – it was more about the fact they couldn't master or control me.

Organising the sponsored walk had made me realise I had strong organisational skills and a flair for achieving results – raising over £1,000 for the Appeal Fund – just by being resourceful; although I subsequently wrestled with my conscience about insulting people with mere money, after they had so heart-breakingly lost loved ones.

By now, I started to appreciate my own management skills and left my contracting role in the south of England and returned closer to home, accepting a Team Leader position with Ericsson's – a telecoms company in Leicester.

I revelled in the responsibility of using creativity to make things happen and my quest for knowledge and learning seemed to be growing exponentially.

After a year, Ericsson's lost the contract and I was left unemployed. Ever-resilient though, I decided to go back to college and do a university Access Course. All my life, people had been telling him how clever I was and now I decided to put it to the test.

In September 1991 – as I approached my 31st birthday – I started full-time at People's College in Nottingham and revelled in the significance of being a mature student and a powerful role model to so many of my younger fellow students.

Part of the academic journey entailed undertaking reflective practice and unsurprisingly, this was something that I particularly enjoyed and excelled at. After all, I'd already been through so much.

This reflective approach took my mind back five months to a totally non-educational event.

Wearing my usual shorts, T-shirt and slippers, I went out one Saturday morning with only a few pence in my pocket to buy a newspaper. As I proceeded to the shop, a mate – driving up Aspley Lane – pulled over and bellowed...

'Are you off to Villa Park tomorrow to see the Reds play against West Ham in the semi?'

'Can't, got no money,' was my simple response.

'No problem – jump in – we'll sort it,' was the rapid retort from Lop, the hopeful driver.

The pair of us spent the day visiting Forest-populated pubs, searching for ways to acquire tickets, which we eventually achieved and proceeded to Villa Park in Birmingham the next day.

Forest won 4-0 – cue a massive drink-related celebration that lasted until the following Wednesday. I turned up back at home some five days later, the worse for drink.

I knocked on my front door, which was duly opened by Bev.

'Where you been?' she angrily enquired.

'The match went into extra-time sweet-heart,' was my attempt at a funny response.

'You stink,' was her damning verdict, commenting on the fact I'd had the same clothes on that I went to the shop in, almost one week earlier.

As the year came to a close, I reflected back to those halcyon days in Bestwood and one of my founding beliefs that the only way out of that hard-fought existence would be sport or education.

After spending so many years fervently believing sport was the primary answer, I smiled to myself as I now started to appreciate the power of learning in its many forms.

This inspired me to pick up the pen and write a poem about one of the most influencing factors in my life so far – the demon drink.

A Question of Bottle

A man in his prison cell, all alone and he's down;
His eyes are all bloodshot and his face wears a frown

One way or another, a life behind bars;
He once had it all, fast money – fast cars

But now he is broken and everything is lost;
The legacy of booze, was it all worth the cost?

He needed his tipple to help him get by;
Now everything's gone, he wished he'd stayed dry

The drink was a comfort when things got too tough;
At night he felt numb, in the morning just rough

The lies and the violence he promised would cease;
But booze had control and never gave peace

Tears stroke his cheeks as he thinks of it now;
Perhaps he would change, if only he knew how?

It's a question of bottle and which one to choose;
The one full of courage or the one full of booze

Neither is easy and both promise gains;
But one offers hope – the other just pains

So when you're alone with only booze as your friend;
Reach out for support – no need to pretend.

A mini phase of reflection continued about how my life had gone from constant pain, suffering and hopelessness – through a process of change – to become someone with an insatiable appetite for learning.

I just wanted to grow more and more.

The emotional whirlwind that often prevailed, instigated tears as my thoughts then flipped over to thinking about the life of duality I had deliberately created.

I had hope though – I'd come to know the power of love.

WOW

We don't know what we don't know. As we raise our awareness though, we become more conscious that there are other ways of being, even if we don't know what they are yet.

My passion for music was starting to flirt with my emotions once again, temporarily rekindled by my all-time favourite tune to Foreigner's *I Want To Know What Love Is* constantly whirling around in my mind.

The lyrics to the ballad reflecting the heartache and pain I had known in my life and how I'd travelled so far to change this lonely life.

Throughout my turbulent life, I had consistently – when in one of my white phases – done many things for charity or the community. Organising the Liverpool walk was my first 'big event' and one I wanted to build on; I had never lost that early-discovered focus of purpose and wanting to serve others.

Whilst at college, I organised a 24-hour sponsored football tournament in early '92, to raise money for three Special Needs Schools in Nottingham.

The new phase of learning wasn't restricted to academia though. I was also starting to become so much more aware of my own emotions – even if it was only in the form of pessimistic self-talk, constantly telling myself how emotionally broke and 'bankrupt' I was.

One thing was becoming clearer however – my marriage to Bev was over. I knew I had a love for her but felt it was more like that of a protective brother, rather than a husband's passion.

Although this was the honest and raw truth, it was still heart-wrenching for me to finally leave the family home and especially, the three most precious gifts in the world – our kids. But I did leave and moved in with a couple of fellow students in spring 1992.

Despite the emotional turbulence of my own precarious childhood, I was determined to shield my own three from any potential negativity, on the back of the split between their parents.

Eight months later, I went on a date with a woman called Les. Wow – the sparks began to fly immediately in every conceivable way!

Although very petite in physical stature, her fiery Latino temperament was a complete contrast to the calming, gentle nature of Bev and one that intrigued me greatly.

I likened my relationship with her to touching wet paint – there was always a warning sign there, but I had to touch it anyway.

On passing my college Access Course, I was offered a place at Nottingham Trent University. Whilst at college, the process I went through dramatically enhanced my own self-worth and gave me a massive surge of confidence, inspiring me writing a poem called 'The Way of Life'.

The Way of Life

Life's paths are littered with many variables. We perceive many things about this enigmatic voyage. Just as we become complacent, the volatile compound of fate and human nature has an uncanny habit of reminding us just how fallible and precarious we are.

Many paradoxes exist – the longer we live, the sooner we die; to enjoy peace, we must be aware of others' wars; though born ignorant, we have potential for wisdom.

Throughout the journey, many different phases evolve which – at the time – we may not enjoy or even understand: but we must rest assured, they are a vital part of our learning & life.

Love is the all-powerful emotion that waters us through the aridity of life's desert. It is the difference between merely existing or living life to the full. It is a reason to carry on and grow; life is a gift and like all gifts, it should be treasured.

Loss comes in many forms, each with their own painful legacy. However, we must always remember as surely as the harsh winter of life kills the beautiful summer flowers, so shall new ones grow again in the spring.

We need many things to survive the turbulent waves of life's sea; but above all we need something to sustain us – knowing in our darkest hours we are not alone – we need faith.

Faith is believing that through all our mistakes and selfishness, we will be forgiven - by ourselves and the universe – and progress to live a life of maximum fulfilment & love.

My newly-increasing confidence was impinged upon though when I received a piece of paper in mid-1993, stating the marriage to Bev was over. This hurt badly – I felt so guilty and regretful of my behaviour towards her.
We'd had ten years together and I fluctuated between an unquenchable thirst for forgiveness, to immeasurable gratitude from having had such a strong and positive, powerful impact in my life.

This forgiveness-gratitude dilemma acted as a domino effect to recalling my errant behaviour in some of my other close relationships – particularly relating to Ma and Win.

I knew I had to take the lessons forward – but not the pain.

> **WOW**
>
> Learn to let go of the pain from the past, but not the lessons learnt.

'WE ALL AGREE... NOTTINGHAM FOREST ARE MAGIC!'

These immortal words echoed from the Lounge of the Royal Oak in Bulwell around to the Bar of the same watering hole. I inquisitively went around to the 'best side' to see who this pretender was to my self-perceived crown of being the next great tenor, following in the same footsteps as Enrico Caruso or Mario Lanza.

There – decked in Forest red – was one John Smith.

'Smudger' as he was predictably labelled, was a well-known, heavily-tattooed character that was equally well-respected. Even though he was very slightly built, he had an infectious and lively spirit; one that under-pinned him constantly raising money for many charitable causes.

He was undoubtedly a rough diamond that initially people were very wary of, but they soon became appreciative of him once they took the trouble to stop outwardly judging him and scratch below the surface.

'Oi, let me show you how to do it!' I buoyantly challenged him.

I was known for my very powerful voice and after delivering a rendition from the opera *Pagliacci*, the pub tendered its applause and duly acknowledged me as the 'winner'.

The irony of the opera was not lost on a local wag as he quipped 'a couple of right clowns together, here'.

'All right then smart-arse, I'll bet I can beat you at drinking,' Smudger half-heartedly offered me.

'Line them up!' was my master tenor's response.

Three double whiskeys and three double Sherries were lined up on the bar for each of the contestants. The barmaid rang the bell and battle commenced, with both of us launching into a rapid 'necking' exercise.

The eventual result – 6-4 to me – was too much for Smudger to accept, forcing him to throw down a desperately-fuelled gauntlet.

'Righto – winner takes all, I'll fight you!'

This was his last-ditch attempt to salvage some much-needed pride. The subsequent humorous rapture from the clientele was enhanced even further by my response.

'That won't be necessary me ol' mucker – I stopped pulling legs off spiders a long time ago'.

This metaphoric olive branch was appreciated by Smudger and laid the solid foundations for a great friendship between us two Forest die-hards.

Upon starting university in autumn 1992, I found it very tough – both academically and practically. Once again, my feelings of deservedness continued to strangle my confidence and part of my constant negative self-chat was 'kids from Bestwood don't go to places like this'.

This simple trigger opened the door for a predicable 'solution' of going on a wild bender again. Two months later, the inevitable dry run kicked in and I transferred my studies to a 2-year HND course at De Montfort University in Leicester – graduating in 1995.

After just over three years of a passionate and drama-filled relationship with Les, we separated. We had spoken about walking away from everything in Nottingham and starting a new life together in Spain.

To allow some reflective time for both of us, I went to Egypt in January 1996 for a week's holiday.

During my time away, I became immersed in an emotional sea of nostalgia – particularly around how fortunate I'd been to have had so much love in my life.

This inspired me write a poem called 'My Love For You'.

> ### My Love for You
>
> *As we travel life's long and winding road, things, we encounter many ordeals. Sometimes, things may happen which we don't understand – like famine, prejudice, injustice and even war. But beyond all of this, there is a gift so precious and warm; a gift so blessed, it gives us the hope and strength to carry on – the gift of love.*
>
> *Love is something I have and feel for you; it is like a deep blue sea – tranquil and beautiful on the surface and yet, with raging undercurrents of unbounded passion underneath. Love is like the sun – radiating warmth and happiness; and like the wind – we cannot see it, merely feel its power.*
>
> *These enigmatic elements change with the seasons, but always remember one thing; something which will ever remain constant – you are so special to me and I will forever love you.*

Yet again, I moved back to live with Ma and Cyril but was determined not to go back on the bottle this time. What I wasn't prepared for though, was a sucker-punch!

A few weeks after the split, Les phoned me and suggested we try again, offering to meet at the same time, day and place we had first met some three years previously – outside Yates's Wine Lodge in Nottingham's City Centre.

I was elated and eagerly looked forward to the grand 'reunion' and touching loads more wet paint! However – as was the way in my chaotic life – nothing ever went to plan.

Such was my happiness at this new opportunity, I decided to leave the confines of my bedroom and take a walk to nearby Bulwell to buy something new; a shirt, aftershave – it didn't matter.

As I reached Bulwell and began to window-shop, I bumped into one of the boys, Gary; he reported how the other guys hadn't seen me for a while and missed me, he then suggested I go for drink with them, now I was here.

'I can't,' I apologetically offered...'I've got a date tonight and need to be tip-top'.

'Don't be an old tart,' Gary joked, continuing 'one won't hurt'.

I knew my all-or-nothing mind-set but rationalised I was strong enough to walk away, even if he ended up having more than one. A few pints later, reminiscing about the 'good old days' the beer began to flow faster and faster.

Then as is the way, one of the loony squad suggested we all went to London to see Forest play in the FA Cup against Spurs.

Like all things when under the influence, it seemed like a good idea at the time. I worked out that if the match finished at 5pm, it'd only take two hours to get back to Nottingham so I'd be okay for my 7 o'clock date.

IDIOT!

The match went into extra time and then penalties – resulting in me getting back to Les's house at nearly midnight, after visiting probably every hostelry on the way back from London.

My giggly drunken elation was not shared by Les. Despite her several attempts to stop my childish ramblings about football, I continued; excitedly sharing with her every kick of the game.

'Here, this'll shut you up,' Les whispered, as she handed me a note.

My misplaced humour immediately ceased, like a juggernaut being stopped in its tracks, instantaneously. The note was badly written but the words were unbelievably powerful and had instant impact.

The up-shot of the content was Les had been totally devoted to me and was prepared to give up everything in Nottingham – her home, job and family – to move to Spain and get married to me.

'That's brilliant,' I excitedly declared.

'You don't understand, you've blown it – it's over,' she reinforced.

Torrents of panic engulfed me as I recollected this was not the first time I'd been delivered such a crushing blow; as Lynne had done all those years before.

Ever hopeful, I had a belief that things could be turned around. After all, we'd been through so much together and this was nothing compared to the previous challenges we'd overcome. Instinctively though, I knew in my heart of hearts, she meant it.

I sank even further as I remembered I'd had exactly the same thoughts where Lynne was concerned and the inevitable outcome. The obvious dawned on me – my beliefs were mine, not other people's; they had their own.

All my emotional pleas fell on stony ground. My male pride had been reduced to that of a little boy asking for his own way.

I got angry with myself for not only being aware of what the obvious cycle of behaviour was; but the fact that I always followed through and never seemed to be able to break this negative pattern.

Throughout all this predictability though, I continued to learn about life and love; taking the proverbial steps forward and then back again and constantly asking myself why was this same cycle of behaviour continuing?

Graduating from De Montfort University with an HND in Engineering meant nothing to me. What did mean everything though, was the introduction to Kaizen, the Japanese continuous improvement philosophy.

Its approach was built on the fact that yesterday's outstanding results will barely suffice for today and be nowhere near good enough for tomorrow. Regardless of all my trials and tribulations, I massively resonated with this and took great inspiration from it.

Fascinated by the legacy of recent academic studies, I wanted to know more. If this principle could be applied to processes, why couldn't it also be applied to people? It was an amazing insight and something that had deeply inspired me to grow more and more.

The usual black phases seemed to trouble me less; it was as if I knew a white – far more potent – replacement would be imminent.

And so it proved.

Just a few weeks after splitting up with Les, I formed a relationship with another beautiful soul. This time with someone that was a lot younger than me and also, she adored my three kids and used to shower them with love and affection every time they came to stay with us.

Laura-Jayne didn't have any kids of her own; but her actions towards my three totally belied any thought she may not have been maternal.

She was a woman of real refinement and her copper-coloured hair nestled at the top of a tall, thin – but curvaceous – body. She had a mental strength that acted as a perfect foil for her sensitive and caring nature.

Around the same time as this new union, I hooked-up with a close pal from my childhood – Billy.

'Hey Paul, how's it going?' asked the long-lost pal from my childhood, as he boarded a bus to the City Centre and walked to sit with me at the back.

'You know, up and down,' I uninspiringly responded.

We spent the twenty-odd minutes of the journey picking up the pieces of our pasts.

The two of us had drifted apart over the years. During my brushes with the law in the mid-late 80's, Billy had become a Prison Warden and in my divisive black & white world of 'us and them' this was unforgiveable.

As kids, we firmly understood what side of the fence we belonged and Billy had crossed over to the other side. But time was a great healer and I began to fleetingly show signs of emotional intelligence and thankfully we became reunited.

Billy and I continued to grow ever-closer. The bond we'd shared as kids clearly hadn't been broken, despite taking contrasting paths in life.

Billy was instrumental in introducing me to the Captain of the Salvation Army where Billy now worked, after being pensioned off from the Prison Service.

The 'Sally Army' wanted to do a big project to bring all their homeless residents together; something that would give them a common goal.

I jumped at the chance and after liaising with the relevant parties, I organised 'The Three Peaks Challenge' which entailed scaling Ben Nevis in Scotland, Sca Fell in England and Snowden in Wales. This time with a difference though – we'd walk the 500 miles in-between.

The 11-day challenge raised over £4,500 for The Salvation Army in south Russia for an area that was decimated by a drugs epidemic.

As I sat on the top of Ben Nevis – enveloped by the misty and awe-inspiring surroundings of this majestic mountain – I committed some thoughts to paper. The words seemed to flow effortlessly – another amazing feat of nature, seeing as I had gone straight into the event on the back of one of my black drinking phases.

Jigsaws

In the stillness and solitude of the night, a man found himself very alone and as a result, began to reflect upon how his life had evolved. He scrutinised many aspects of his past experiences and became conscious of the fact he had deliberately acknowledged his achievements but ignored his downfalls.

Physically, he recalled the prowess of his youth – his yearning spirit to 'kiss the sun & touch the moon' – and how he had won the majority of life's battles & races and achieved many goals. He tensed his body as he reassured himself he still had a Herculean-like physique.

Mentally, he enthused over his many academic achievements; how he had helped many people secure gainful employment by building successful companies & communities. Emotionally, he relived the many joyous events he had been involved in; his close, loving family and the respect of a vast array of people.

However, these smiles of contentment soon turned to tears of sadness as a more realistic and painful recollection began to evolve; recalling the people he had once loved, but ultimately ended-up losing, due to his fragility. He likened these different aspects of his life to pieces in a jigsaw, which –when all fitted together – gave him a more complete picture of his polarised and turbulent life.

This led him to realise that something was missing; as he began to experience a great sense of regret and insecurity and tears stroked his cheeks as a testimony to his hurt & pain. This new-found awareness gave him great cause for concern and forced him to question his beliefs on religion and spirituality; and what these words even meant?

He found relative peace in the realisation that everyone's life is made up of different phases and experiences; but without the stability of something to rest them upon they will simply fall apart and become meaningless.

As a result, a new phase of emergence began to unfold; providing a foundation for faith and allowing all the different pieces of his life to fit together—like a jigsaw upon a table — to give his life meaning and purpose; his spiritual journey had begun.

'What's up wit' you lad?'

Irish Mick growled at me as the two of us sat in the Dog & Partridge drinking on a Friday when – at five minutes to mid-day – I shivered uncontrollably for a few seconds and made Mick spill his drink.

'Dunno Michael,' I apologetically responded, before continuing…

'Something's happened and it's not good!'

We continued our drinking session until I returned home later that night, where I informed Laura-Jayne of my eerie experience at lunchtime.

Less than 48 hours later, the phone rang.

'Aren't you going to answer it?' Laura-Jayne enquired.

My subconscious mind automatically diverted my thoughts back to that same immortal question that Bev had asked of me all those years ago.

I intuitively knew the conclusion would be the same now, as it was then – bad news – and I was right.

'Billy's dead!' A female voice uttered as I answered the phone. I instinctively put the phone down – without a response.

'Are you going out?' Laura-Jayne asked gently.

She knew me and was well aware – from both the conversations and the experiences we'd shared – of how I always reacted to any black challenges. She realised her question was futile.

Barely two years after our reunion, Billy had committed suicide. He'd constantly propounded to me about his '7-year hitch' and how he believed the breakdown he'd previously experienced would happen again, every seven years; this became his self-fulfilling prophecy.

The pressure of expectation and wanting to achieve things was too much for him and the inevitable breakdown occurred.

> **WOW**
>
> Alternative suggestion - Nothing weighs heavier on yourself or others than the weight of expectations.

One thing I had become very adept at though was picking up shattered pieces of my life and despite the emotional turmoil relating to Billy's passing, I knew I would eventually fight my way through it.

As the new millennium approached, there was a definite shift occurring in my thoughts; I was starting to think much more strategically.

The epitome of this was the realisation that the Teaching Degree I would be starting, was only a stepping stone for me to study what I was really passionate about – continuous improvement.

The two-year academic journey no longer held any of my feelings of deservedness that had previously prevailed five years earlier, when going to university for the first time.

I was beginning to really embrace my role as a leader and more importantly, a social leader.

One of the things that I had focused on as a youngster was being involved with the youth set-up at Nottingham Forest Football Club, as an apprentice footballer.

Some twenty four years later, I became involved with the club – as a mentor.

Whilst working through my Teaching Degree, I had secured a part-time position as a Learning Mentor to some of the best young talent in football.

I worked with 16-18 year-old apprentices in Nottingham Forest's prestigious Academy – mainly on their education and mindsets – helping them learn and grow as they pursued their career in football.

Whilst there, I became very active in organising fund-raising activities through a group I formed, called Football ACTS (Assisting Communities Through Sport).

I set this up with one simple goal: to help people less fortunate than ourselves.

What initially started out as a bit of fun, grew very quickly, with tens of thousands of pounds being raised for national charities like Sargent Cancer Care For Children and The Guide Dogs For The Blind; this being supplemented by twice undertaking a two-week bike ride around selected football clubs in England.

Within a matter of weeks of the new millennium, three things of significance happened.

I got my degree, totally dispelling my previously-held belief that Bestwood boys don't go to university.

Also, I shook hands with the Duke of Edinburgh when the Prince officially opened the Study Centre at Nottingham Forest, where I worked as a mentor.

Thirdly, I met Les Bradd for the first time.

This being the very same Les Bradd – Notts County Football Club's all-time record goal-scorer – that had scored the winning goal against Forest some twenty five years ago. At the time that goal had reduced me to tears and made me hate 'Bomber Bradd' with all my heart.

Les had become Commercial Manager at Forest and – although an unlikely pairing – we soon struck up a good understanding between us, which progressed onto become a strong friendship.

Physically, Les was a stereotypical old-fashioned centre-forward – tall, thick-set with big powerful legs. He had a natural confidence about him, but without any trace of arrogance or ego; he was a gentleman and a real positive influence in my life.

The two of us often joked about our Scorpio birth sign and how we both had an all-or-nothing attitude and commitment to the game of life.

Such was the positive impact that Football ACTS was having – benefitting many different causes – I was now starting to believe I had uncovered my true vocation in life; it fitted in with the belief that my purpose was to serve less fortunate souls in the world.

I knew from an early age I was very different from all my peers, but the labels of 'odd ball,' 'crazy' and even 'psycho' never bothered me.

I accepted from that fateful day back in March 1974 that I had a purpose in life and nothing was going to stop me, even though I was still struggling with my demons.

> ### WOW
>
> Even though my demons were still very apparent, at least I had the self-awareness to recognise and acknowledge them.
>
> This is a vital step to healing.

Building on the successes of ACTS, I liaised with my trusty team and asked them what they thought about becoming a proper charity. ACTS had only ever started as a bit of fun and no one ever fore-saw it progressing to achieve the significantly positive things it did.

This sparked an emotional reaction in me, as I asked myself 'how can a boy from Bestwood form a charity and do all these good things – it doesn't make sense?'

Overcoming my self-doubt, SportACTS was formed – a registered Charity Trust – and the good works continued. As the charity's achievements became bigger and bigger, this seemed to magnify the duality in my world.

To the outside, I was a strong, focussed leader – benefitting those less fortunate – but inside, I felt I was living a massive lie. Why did I have to put on this smoke-screen of being a tough, hard-drinking no-nonsense character?

This question was never far away from my consciousness but nonetheless, me and the team continued our fund-raising exploits and continued to serve some great national charities such as Childline, CP Sport, DARE (Drug Awareness Resistance Education), Kidney Research and many more local community initiatives, including an annual bike ride to Liverpool to commemorate the 96 that tragically lost their lives in the Hillsborough Disaster.

As my profile began to rise – I was often interviewed by various media – I regularly flirted with guilt and anger.

Initially, I had revelled in the notoriety and the significance all these very worthwhile initiatives had given me, but then selfishly – so I thought – started to ask myself more and more 'but who's helping me?'

My black & white conditioning was extremely ingrained and I desperately craved change – but how?

WOW

Part of any growth and development is the ability to ask ourselves the right questions.

Ask yourself better questions and your mind will automatically search for quality answers and solutions.

This question was never far from my thoughts and in my mind, I used the concept of a boxer constantly jabbing away – looking for that knock-out moment – believing that sooner or later the right answer would appear and I would be able to conquer this all-powerful 'opponent' once and for all.

I was consoled by reassuring myself that at least I was responsible for doing a lot of good things, whilst I continued to search for that elusive solution.

Externally, the accomplishments continued to flow. I achieved my strategic goal of a Master's Degree from the prestigious Nottingham Business School, in 2002.

I'd been living with Laura–Jayne since the mid-90's and she had been brilliantly supportive of me – both financially and emotionally. I was now 41 years old and after spending more than a decade in academia – it was now time for me to go back to work

As was the way in my thinking, there were no free rides in life for me or anyone and I saw this as an opportunity to start to pay back the colossal moral debt that I perceived I owed her.

I became an auditor – checking contractor's cable jointing work – covering the Anglia area and undertook a six-hour round trip each day from Nottingham to Norwich or Ipswich. The time-consuming tedium of all this travelling was not lost on me.

During my extensive fund-raising exploits, I had learnt how to become resourceful to achieve many goals.

This intuitive and entrepreneurial way – often flying by the seat of my pants – was a million miles away from the monotony and drudgery of being stuck in a car for most of the day; it reminded him of my time as a taxi driver.

Also, this time-for-money approach just didn't feel right; but for the time being, it was all I knew.

As had consistently been the way throughout most of my life – apart from early childhood – the demon drink was always alert to seize an opportunity to enter my world and create havoc, like a cowardly bully looking to strike on an unsuspecting victim.

In my own mind, that's what I had come to believe – that I was a victim.

The catalyst for my next bout of boozing was the news that I'd been diagnosed with diabetes.

Doing the daily Anglia run had lasted for a few months which had confirmed for me that I only wanted to work for myself; or as part of a team that shared a common goal of making life better for people less fortunate. This inspired an idea – I would get involved with taxiing again; but this time, I'd run my own taxi firm. I was greatly enthused at this prospect; it embraced some of my social leader values, such as helping people earn a living.

This new initiative wasn't meant to be though. Upon going for the obligatory medical, the doctor duly informed me I wouldn't be granted a licence because of the diabetes diagnosis.

'What's this diabetes thing?' I innocently enquired, listening intently but frustratingly to the doctor's insight and the strong suggestion that the years of heavy drinking had contributed to acquiring this condition.

I hated losing at anything and the rejection of this licence was perceived as a loss – such was my black & white mind-set.

> ## WOW
>
> In times of stress we often default to our previous conditioning – it's hard to shake the foundations we are built on.

'That's all right, I'm not bothered about the licence – but I'll beat the diabetes one day!' was my defiant reply to the doctor.

Predictably, this opened the door for another binge and it was on this particular bout that a Good Samaritan came to my rescue – for the third time.

A few days into another one of my self-destruct missions, I – along with a couple of other fellow drinkers – staggered from pub to pub in Nottingham's lively City Centre.

A dimly-lit short cut alleyway between Parliament Street and Angel Row provided the stage for my latest escapade.

One of my loud-mouthed drinking buddies Martin couldn't resist the opportunity to bait three youths that walked towards us. Despite my attempts to diffuse the situation, all hell broke loose between the six of us – broken only by a stranger yelling 'scarper, the coppers are on their way!'

Bloodied and bruised, the three of us entered the nearby Yates's Wine Lodge. I was pals with a couple of the doormen there and as we settled down with a drink inside the pub, Martin admiringly said to me...'Bloody hell mate, that was impressive; where did you do your ninja training?'

I was in no mood for his quips and misplaced attempts at humour – which reflected by my curt and angry response to him...

'Shut it, you could have got us killed there, shouting off that big mouth of yours!'

Martin submissively responded...

'I know mate and I'm sorry, but the way you did that forward roll just as that geezer was about to chop the back of your head with a machete was amazing – you must have eyes in the back of your head'.

I could tell by Martin's whole body language that he was serious. The reality was the would-be ninja wasn't aware of any of this. What I was conscious of though was an 'unknown force' had propelled me forward so that I landed on my feet, enabling me to emerge victorious against the potential slayer.

The remaining four testosterone-fuelled males were stunned into inaction for a few seconds until the stranger's police warning dispersed us all.

As time continued to roll on, my predictable black & white existence prevailed and the new millennium was barely five years old before three very significant things had happened.

Firstly, the legendary Brian Clough had passed in 2004.

The effect that this iconic father-figure had on me was immeasurable. I loved Brian's brash, opinionated and confident style that the enigmatic football genius seemed to exude; sensing – rightly or wrongly – this belied a far more caring and loving man underneath.

Such was my love and respect for Brian – and how the great man had influenced my life over the years – that I wrote to the Clough family, asking them for permission to organise a charity fund-raising dinner in Brian's honour; promising I would raise at least £20,000 for charity.

I was overwhelmed with joy when I received a phone call from Brian's eldest son Simon, confirming the family's approval of such an event.

My sheer elation was equally shared by Ma as she emotionally tendered...'I'm so proud of you son – I know what Brian meant to you and I'm so sorry for not ever giving you the loving father you deserved'.

More than anything Ma and me had ever experienced together, this single statement from her moved us both to a place of unsurpassed connection. We hugged each other and cried together for what seemed an eternity, eventually releasing to witness the tears of pure love on each other's faces.

The Beast – in all his sickening, twisted and depraved acts – could not destroy our bond and the imminent fund-raising event would be a moment that only Ma and I would ever truly know the significance of.

Apart from my pre-teenage years, Ma and I had never had a serious heart-to-heart and certainly never shared tears of joy together – until now. Pragmatic as ever though, I parked all emotion, and began the serious task of organising the event.

One of my first tasks – as I became heavily embroiled in all the details associated with organising a 'perfect night' for nearly 600 people – was to reserve two complimentary tickets for Ma.

It was difficult to establish which one of us experienced the most excitement about the imminent fund-raiser – her or me?

A lot of high-profile guests from the world of sport – particularly from Forest's halcyon days – confirmed their attendance.

Then TRAGEDY!

With barely seven weeks to go before 'The Brian Clough Tribute Dinner,' Ma died.

At the relatively young age of 64, she died of lung cancer; just as her mother Win before her, due to many years' of heavy smoking.

I took no comfort from recalling Ma's assertion that her nips of whiskey and sherry – along with the cigarettes – were her ways of coping with The Beast's evil antics.

I was in complete meltdown – I wanted to kill the evil bastard that had deprived this beautiful matriarchal soul from the life of love and happiness that she absolutely deserved.

True to form, my black default behaviour wanted to kick-in.

As much as I reassured myself that I had always been able to pull something out the bag when it mattered most, I instinctively knew that if I screwed this event up all my hard-earned confidence and credibility would be destroyed – forever.

This realisation was reinforced even more strongly by something that was said to me after my grandma Win died; by Mo, the mother to one of my football mates.

'Bury your dead!' Mo wisely advised me, continuing...'Your grandma loved you with all her heart and the last thing she would have wanted, is to see you in this constant turmoil – bury your dead and Let It Go!'

WOW

Even though this was excellent advice – recognising its importance – the need for control still lingered.

Three of the most important words in life – 'Let It Go'.

After Win's death, I'd carried on in victim mode for years to the point where I even believed she was part of the reason for my erratic existence. My more rational thoughts totally dismissing this as an insulting lie.

The reality was, my demise was always somebody else's fault – never my own – and in those days I wouldn't take responsibility for my actions, especially those associated with the black side of life.

History seemed as though it was going to repeat itself, the only difference this time, was I remembered Mo's wise words.

Over recent years, I had told myself that the next time I lost someone really close, I would grieve up until the moment they were buried or cremated – then after that, it would be over.

And so it was. Ten days after Ma's death, she was laid to rest in a family plot at Bulwell Cemetery – alongside Win and Grandad Jack, who had died before I was born.

The cruel irony of her premature demise was that she passed away on The Beast's birthday.

All the recollections of Win, Billy and Ma seemed to galvanise me to the point where I consciously parked my emotions and got on with the task in-hand and was even more committed to making the Tribute Dinner an overwhelming success.

The sense of achievement that I felt afterwards was immeasurable, with over £22,000 raised for many local charitable causes in Derby and Nottingham.

Even though the obligatory 'happy' celebration ensued, I was under no illusion this was just a curtain that veiled a more underlying, realistic truth; I had a serious drink problem and some very deep-rooted psychological issues and I needed help – fast!

Engaging with local support agencies to seek a remedy, I found them an unnatural match and knew that the answer to my challenges lay within me, fervently believing I had the strength to find a solution – but how?

I wasn't the only one with a bad illness. Laura-Jayne was experiencing constant falls and was subsequently diagnosed with the hereditary-influenced Muscular Dystrophy (MD).

Between us, we devised a plan that would help alleviate her challenges. It was decided that I would buy the existing house off Laura-Jayne and she could then use the capital to purchase a more MD-friendly bungalow.

My entrepreneurial activities meant I received a good income, I organised Black Tie events, Golf Days and I also owned a small memorabilia business.

I raised a mortgage on the property and Laura-Jayne proceeded to buy her new property. With the first goal achieved, the next stage was to sell my newly-acquired property and the two of us would then live in the bungalow.

Great plan, but a big bomb-shell then ensued!

'I can't do it – I don't love you anymore,' was Laura-Jayne's revelation.

She explained how she had deliberated for weeks, on how to break the news to me, fearful it would be the trigger for yet another dark spell in my life. She needn't have bothered. My insensitive and equally bland response to her was...'No problem, I understand'.

There was a massive problem though – I'd lied. I simply didn't understand; I was only vaguely beginning to know my own world, let alone others.

Because I was essentially an entrepreneur, I had no one to answer to work-wise. I'd become very confident in my resourcefulness to always secure a good income and used this belief to fund time away in a place that I had come to love with a passion – Spain.

After the split, I sold the property and went off to Benidorm for a few months, where – despite wine, women & song prevailing – I engaged in some deep reflections.

Whilst the demon drink was a very black 'relationship' in my life, I was determined not to let it dominate my thoughts, feelings or perceptions.

Part of this reflective phase encompassed how fortunate I had been with the women-folk in my life. In their own respective ways, they had all been monumental to my survival, inspiration and growth.

As I approached my half-century of life, I self-challenged and deduced that a lot of people had shown me oceans of love, and I had reciprocated to an army of people through my life-enhancing charity work.

But there were still big question to be answered...'what about me – why didn't I have self-love?

Maybe this was at the heart of all my dark years, I self-quizzed. Maybe my beliefs were all wrong?

WOW

Another major step forward – where else had my
beliefs not served me?

'So what about me?'

I asked myself this question over and over again. By now, I started to really become immersed in the teachings and philosophies of many of the world's leading personal development practitioners.

Becoming aware of the Kaizen continuous improvement approach certainly had an ever-growing effect on me and I wanted to know more;

BINGO!

After months of painstaking research, a breakthrough came.

All the various mentors made reference to love and how it made the world go round. I searched for proof, which was quickly reinforced by memories of the masses of love songs I had listened to in my younger days – they can't all be wrong, I reassured myself.

One song though, particularly struck a chord with me, louder than any other.

George Benson's 'Greatest Love Of All...' the lyrics reverberated through my mind and especially the references to children being the future; searching for someone to look up to and most importantly, finding that elusive love inside.

'THAT'S IT – INSIDE – IT'S ALL ABOUT ME!'

I yelled as if there was a packed-filled arena awaiting an important announcement. There wasn't – I was alone, in the bath.

'Learning to love yourself is the greatest love of all'...I enthusiastically continued singing, whilst simultaneously realising that all my life, I had given away my emotional power.

My previously besotted attachment to Nottingham Forest started to dominate my thoughts. The fact I had given them so much emotional energy over the years was really a smokescreen for not feeling worthy of self-love – which was definitely the result of The Beast's influence on me.

This was a monumental moment, knowing the time had come for me to start emerging from the Forest – my black & white years of being lost in the wilderness were over.

My elation at this immeasurable breakthrough temporarily became challenged as it dovetailed into my age-old dilemma – but how?

This formidable nemesis seemed to fade into relative insignificance though. I now knew what I was dealing with; the hard part had been done – or so I thought!

Whilst my views about love were committed to paper – when I was on holiday alone on the African continent, at a time when Les and I had separated – I had never become as expressive verbally.

106

I had never declared to any of my 'special ladies' how much I adored and loved them. Although I felt secure enough to share my vulnerability with them, this didn't extend to uttering the three time-honoured words they loved and appreciated hearing. This was about to dramatically change though.

Maybe the reason up until now, was that I hadn't recognised the importance of loving myself first?

PART THREE:

LIVING LIFE
ON PURPOSE

The New Year of 2010 appeared and **as** it was going to be my 50th birthday in the autumn, I recalled how the previous two years had unfolded, with a host of life-changing experiences. As well as splitting up from Laura-Jayne, selling the house and spending months in Benidorm, I'd also wound-up SportActs.

As part of my need for certainty and control, I had been in the driver's seat of all the charity's activities over its six-year duration and as a consequence, had burned myself out. Having not prepared for anyone else to take my place, the charity folded.

Despite that, I gleaned an immense amount of satisfaction from its monumental achievements and was full of gratitude to the team, for all their individual and collective contributions.

SportActs – like its predecessor Football ACTS – had raised six-figure amounts for many charitable initiatives. I took vital time out to reflect upon many lessons learnt and now felt re-energised, ready to start a new, bigger project.

Now back in the UK and hungry for success – I prioritised three massive goals.

Firstly, I set strong intentions to finally address the demon drink once and for all; secondly, to find a new partner and thirdly, to start a new charity.

The continuous improvement philosophy was never far from my mind and I now believed the time had come to really commit and put it into practise.

I didn't have to wait long for the first two opportunities to arrive. Firstly on January 3rd, I was delivered a knock-out punch when I met Lyn – a Relationship Transformation Expert – who also had a strong Spanish connection; her mother Maureen lived in Spain.

The ironies of life never ceased to amaze me, with her mother living a stone's throw from where Doug (my father) had also settled in Spain.

Lyn had a curvaceous Latino look about her and we had a deep soul connection from the start. Her beautiful Spanish-looking appearance being a perfect foil for her pretty green eyes. Being my typical type, she instantly captured my heart.

She had a happy, bubbly laid-back personality and I felt compelled to sweep her off her feet with all the masculine passion I could muster.

It worked! She melted and somehow she immediately saw the real me beneath my fake hard nut exterior. It wasn't long before I began to feel that begin to crack!

Spiritually, we shared and confided our personal harrowing stories and spent endless hours - excitingly talking about personal development and how we wanted to create a legacy for the world. I also remember that one of our theme tunes at the time was – *You Make Me Feel Brand New* by The Stylistics.

The deep love we shared and this common goal proved to be immensely powerful glue between us as the early stages of our relationship presented significant challenges. I was wrestling to shake off my aggressive fake no-nonsense persona and Lyn did not yet know me as well as she does now in order to respond without causing things to escalate.

Such was my happiness though – because I'd achieved my first goal – I decided to celebrate, by having a drink!

As one that never did things by halves, my little celebration tipple lasted three whole weeks - with the lads in the pub sick to the back teeth of hearing about the new love in my life - it only came to an end when I faced a stark realisation – I strongly believed I was going to die.

The reality was, years of physical and psychological abuse to the body and mind had taken its toll. As I lay bed-ridden for days – going through cold turkey withdrawal – I knew things would be different if I pulled through.

As well as my body feeling virtually lifeless, I agonisingly experienced violent nightmares and my nerves were completely shot to pieces, I craved the 'fix' of another drink but knew it was futile.

Just like the previous years with the pneumonia experience, I wouldn't allow the intervention of a doctor; my ego insisted that nature would take its course.

After several touch-and-go moments, I managed to slowly come around and as I did so, I realized the battle with the demon drink was finally over for good. It didn't have anything left to offer me.

A lot of my past associates had addictions – either with alcohol, drugs or both – and they'd all advised me that I would only ever be able to take one day at a time.

'BOLLOCKS!' was my stock-in-trade response whenever I subsequently bumped into any of them, defiantly following up with…'Life may only give us one moment at a time but I'm telling you now, I'll never touch the stuff again'.

WOW
Our internal self-talk is critical; it re-affirms our intentions and in my case, showed that I had moved beyond those external crutches that I'd previously relied on.

Another thing that I had often cogitated, was the abrupt way the relationship with Laura-Jayne had ended – it just didn't make sense.

Amid one of my many conversations with Lyn, I relayed the perceived premature ending with my copper-colour haired ex-girlfriend.

Lyn knowingly shook her head and stated…'You guys just don't have a clue, do you?'

Still none the wiser, I asked for clarity.

Lyn simply went on to explain…'Because of her illness, she was feeling vulnerable and insecure. She needed to know her man would be there for her – regardless.

'A woman in love will always test her man to see if he's worthy of her love. She wanted you to fight for her and you failed – hands down!'

I was confused and asked her...'why didn't she just ask me to stick by her?'

Lyn just shook her head in mock disbelief and playfully rolled her eyes.

As I saw it, I was now 2-0 up in the game of life – with Lyn and sobriety – I now had a third, match-winning goal in my sights. I formed Sporting HEARTS CIC a few days before my 50th birthday in October 2010.

I assembled a team of players that I anticipated would be totally committed to making life better for others and working towards the HEARTS vision and acronym of:

Helping Everyone Achieve Results Towards Success.

I gave deep thought to the president's role and who had the necessary values to fill this honorary position. As a result, I approached Paul Hart, the ex- Forest Academy director and Club Manager.

Harty – as he was affectionately known – had a reputation and respect for investing in youth, which was second-to-none and so it inspired great enthusiasm for the task ahead, when he accepted the position and was instrumental in the charity's progression for a couple of years, until his football commitments made it impossible for him to continue.

Despite him reluctantly stepping down, Sporting HEARTS continued to progress and rolled out many significant life-enhancing projects.

As well as emerging from the metaphoric forest that I had kept myself imprisoned in for so many years, I now totally embraced the desire to break free from the debilitating emotional wilderness that I had become attached to – it was now time to 'Let It Go'.

It was time to swap my love for the game of football for a far bigger, more global arena and become a star performer in the game of life, instead.

Funny how history repeats itself, I mused, as I packed my bags ready to start a new life in sunny Spain, in early 2013. For many years, I'd wanted to live there.

I loved their mañana approach to life and knew – from my many previous stints there – how therapeutic and beneficial this relaxed way of life was to people's health and well-being; accepting that a simple, natural approach to life did not necessitate great amounts of financial wealth to sustain.

Newly-arrived there, Lyn and I began our exciting journey together with endless conversations about how we could make a significant difference to the world. We talked incessantly about the fact this would only manifest by each of us being the very best we could be, as individuals.

Our individual and collective journeys of continuous improvement were ongoing – this being inspired by some of the world's greatest personal development and relationship practitioners. I constantly listened intently to CDs galore, watched videos + DVDs and totally consumed self-help learning – online and through live events.

As I started to relax and enjoy this new chapter of life, I likened it to being on a journey from pain to purpose, recalling many contrasting experiences along the way.

The difference this time though, was I was not attached to the end result.

I had learned many things along his colourful trek; one of them being events in life are neutral, they only have the emotional power and meaning we give them. I learned to focus on taking action, but not be attached to the outcome, whatever that may be.

One of the things I had struggled with – for almost all of my life – had been deservedness and particularly self-recognition.

'We're eating out tonight girl,' I buoyantly asserted to Lyn.

'Why, what's the special occasion, not that there needs to be one,' she quipped.

'I'm free!'

I joyfully exclaimed, having just come off the phone and speaking to the doctor about my annual diabetes test results; recounting my pledge to another doctor – over a decade previously – that I would beat this debilitating disease.

It felt like I was taking back control of everything I had relinquished throughout my life, emerging from the forest as the victor – not a victim.

> **WOW**
> The key to this transformation, is don't worry about or try to control things which are out of your control.

This new identity inspired me greatly. What an unrecognisable difference to my previous label as an aggressive hard-drinking fighter. I intuitively knew the latter was a complete lie – I'd known this for years but if ever I needed a final confirmation that I had lived a life of duality, my old negative perceived self soon became banished, once and for all, at the age of 54 in 2015.

'Tell him Amy,' I politely requested of my now grown-up daughter, referring to her new Border Collie, Maxwell – as the black & white canine sat intently and stared unflinchingly at me, with his beautiful, piercing blue eyes.

'He loves you dad,' Amy unreservedly responded, adding…'that's why he's looking at you and he knows you love him too' my proud daughter concluded.

'I'll wait for you in the car,' I abruptly and emotionally responded, as I broke eye contact with Maxwell.

A couple of minutes later, Amy joined me and posed the question…'you alright dad?' further adding…'I've never seen my hard-man dad all emotional, like this'.

'And that's the problem,' I apologetically mustered, before adding…'all my life, I've been living a lie – a life of duality'.

The concerned daughter was clearly confused.

'I don't understand,' she muttered, before I tried to explain.

'When I witnessed Maxwell's powerful blue eyes staring at me, it took me back to when I was a kid of seven and I had a playful black & white mongrel called Rocky'.

I steadied myself before clarifying...'he was my world and made me so happy and complete'.

I continued to explain that once The Beast had come into my life, I had to change my world to survive. Seeing Maxwell restored my awareness of who I truly was – a caring, loving soul.

As I began to regain composure, I reflected upon the whole, tortuous journey and it made perfect sense to conclude that although I was prepared to take on everybody else's fight and struggles, I'd ignored the most critical one of all – my own.

My physical, mental and emotional health had been neglected and it was time to redress the balance. The question of self-love triggered my consciousness around self-forgiveness and self-gratitude – these too had been overlooked.

Being a victim at the hands of The Beast was something that prevailed for far too many years in my life and something that I was reminded of, as a result of an out-of-the-blue phone call from Smudger – my old 'opera' singing partner and Forest pal.

'Psycho, I've got something I want you to do for me,' Smudger excitedly ordered. These opening words threw me on two counts. Firstly, I had forgotten the nickname he had given me from our Forest exploits together. Secondly, there were no introductory pleasantries – reasonable to expect after so long apart?

Smudger mumbled on about organising a Scottish Piper for a funeral he would imminently be attending, as I semi-apologetically dismissed his long-lost pal's request.

As the conversation unfolded, I was reminded of a similar shiver-like experience I'd once had, when receiving news about Billy's passing.

'When I get back to Blighty, I'll come and see you – you still at Top Valley?'

I enquired. No sooner had I finished asking the question, I felt my body quiver for a few seconds, just as it had done way back in 1998.

'Nah, I'm at Basford now,' Smudger offered.

'Don't tell me, Pear Tree Court?' I curiously enquired.

'Yep!' was the simple response.

'Number twenty-one?' I further probed.

'Yep, how did you know?' Smudger concluded.

'I'll tell you when I see you,' was my response.

Following dialogue that was dominated by tales of 'the good old days,' I promised I'd visit my old Forest mate the next time I was back in the UK.

True to my word – a few weeks later – I eerily re-visited the same flat that Win had lived in all those years ago. Memories abounded – I steeled myself, careful to not let my emotions show to my old pal. After all, big boys don't cry – do they?

After the nostalgia-filled pair of us spent time catching up, I asked if we could take a walk in the garden area.

'Why?' a perplexed Smudger asked.

As we proceeded to the aforementioned garden area, I went into a contemplative silence. Smudger had seen me like this many times before and knew not to interfere – he just let me be.

'Wait there!'

I ordered a few yards from a five-foot holly-clad wall, before I proceeded alone to look over it.

'JUSTICE!' I cried out to my long-time ally, continuing...'come and have a look at this'.

Smudger similarly proceeded to the wall and couldn't believe his eyes, reacting...'fuckin' hell Psycho, it's like Fort Knox!'

The pair of us observed a property that was heavily adorned with grilles and bars on the windows, padlocks on the doors and spikes on the fences.

Initial observations may have drawn a stranger to conclude the simple two up-two down property was housing the Crown Jewels; it wasn't – it was the dwelling of...

THE BEAST!

WOW

People come and go in our lives and we can learn something from each and every one of those experiences – no matter how challenging they may seem at the time.

For me, I now had the validation that I had overcome The Beast by not being like him – I had passed that test and moved on.

Horrific thoughts temporarily flashed through my mind – re-living one hellish experience after another – and none more so that my previous default coping mechanism of the demon drink.

'Why you smiling Psycho?'

Smudger bemusedly asked me, before quipping...'it's enough to drive a man to drink'.

'Yep, it did and that's why I'm smiling – I've learnt to leave it all behind, unlike The Beast'.

'It's Karma, Psycho,' Smudger wittingly suggested.

Health had always been at the forefront of my mind, from a young age – probably down to my belief that sport would one day provide escapism from the stark reality of my early life – even though the experiences from the ensuing years provided inconsistent evidence to back it up.

But that was history now and I knew progress would always be based upon letting go of the pain from the past – but not the lessons learnt.

Letting go had become an everyday part of my focus now and that included the one thing that had dominated my life for the last six years – Sporting HEARTS.

The charity had positively affected the lives of over 3,000 young people during the six year period from its formation in 2010 – but my ever-increasing awareness showed me I had to adjust to the constantly moving goalposts.

The stepping stones of advancement were not lost on me – even if I had forgotten the price paid for such progression – as I proudly enthused over the significant achievements of Football ACTS, SportACTS and more recently, Sporting HEARTS.

I learnt key lessons each time before developing a new subsequent entity that would reach out and positively affect even more people; and at a deeper level.

This time – on the back of exponential-type learning and growth for me – Sporting HEARTS was wound up in early 2017, making way for HEARTS Global, with a purpose of:

> *Offering life opportunities to vulnerable and disadvantaged people – helping them tackle issues such as abuse and addiction, gang crime and homelessness – to progress to a life of independence and prosperity.*

I pictured my life as a metaphoric puzzle and – as time passed – I fitted more and more pieces together to add to the picture, just like a jigsaw.

I imagined how different pieces could have created a completely contrasting picture. What would my life have been like if Ma hadn't entered into that ill-fated second marriage?

What about if I hadn't endured long-term pain and suffering – would I still have had his vision to leave the world a better place? I thought about how things may have turned out if:

- ❖ I hadn't attempted to end things in 1974. Would I have made a vow to never fly again or become a victim? Would I have committed to a lifetime journey of Learning?

- ❖ I hadn't made the decision in 1991 to take another significant step on my learning voyage; discovered self-awareness and the importance of Loving?

- ❖ I hadn't formed the Sporting HEARTS charity in 2010 and latterly HEARTS Global – positively affecting thousands of people's lives – contributing to leave a world-wide Legacy?

Today, my awareness manifests itself in the work I do as a mentor – Helping Everyone Achieve Results Towards Success – as I constantly strive to meet my own desire for contribution and transformation.

I know the past cannot be changed, but I also accept it contains some very colourful pieces that can be used to create a new – more empowering – future picture for each and everyone one of us.

I did just that with my 'Three Pillars of Life' approach; starting out by believing my life had been one 'L' of a journey and concluded by thinking, it could be summed up very succinctly by 3L's:

Learning | Loving | Legacy.

'So what would be your legacy?' Lyn asked of me.

'That's simple, to leave it all behind,' I responded.

'Leave what behind?' she probed further.

'Two things,' I quickly responded, before elaborating: 'Firstly, leaving the pain from the past behind – but not the lessons learnt'.

'The second one?' she asked.

'To leave a better world behind,' I passionately responded.

> ## WOW
>
> This was a strong affirmation that I had well and truly emerged from the dark forest and into the radiant, light – for good.

Throughout my journey – from pain to purpose – there have been many influential factors. For example, I have come to understand the immense power of words – particularly in the context of the story we tell ourselves about our lives – and how they are an all-potent reflection of who we feel we are, in any given moment of time.

The use of metaphors is also an incredibly powerful tool to help us progress. Indeed in this story, the title of the book is meant to convey how I have emerged from the Forest – Nottingham Forest – after being totally (emotionally) attached to every result they achieved.

Although I still have an emotive connection to the football club, I am no longer lost in them – I have reclaimed my control and power; making the switch to now help others plant acorns so that they may grow their own forests, rather than be part of someone else's.

To continue the football metaphor, I was previously a very defensive-minded, cynical player; my early life's experiences had taught me to play dirty and use any tactic that ensured winning at all costs.

Having become so embroiled in this way of thinking, I became totally unaware of reality. However, the harsh facts were, 'winning' was merely a smokescreen for raw, brutal survival and the price I paid was extremely high.

My mind-set today is far more creative and forward-thinking because I now have the confidence to lead players that are hungry for success and aspire to achieve many worthy goals.

I mentor people that are searching for their life's purpose, with a very clear message: you don't have to pay the ludicrously elevated price I did, to master the game of life.

One of the questions I often get asked is 'how will you achieve all the things you want to, and leave the world a better place?'

My answer is simple – I have only just started the 'second-half' of the match in my game of life.

The first-half (50+ years) was all about me learning how to master the game as a player. Now it's about me passing on those lessons as a coach and mentor, for as long as the higher powers deem appropriate.

From my own perspective, I am totally prepared and focused on lasting the full duration of the 'game' which could be 90-plus – minutes or years – who cares?

Creative thinking – united with unshakeable self-belief – is a very powerful formula for success in life.

Whilst to some, this may be deemed as 'crazy thinking' it was the game-changing Steve Jobs that coined the phrase 'the people that are crazy enough to think they can change the world are the ones that do'.

Interesting as I look back on this story I've written and – upon reflection – whether an alternative title for the book may have been:

'My Purpose Is To Leave The World A Better Place – What's Yours?'

I may only be small and vulnerable - like so many other souls in this world - but as I continue to grow, I will contribute to make the world a better place

PaulLoweHEARTS

Epilogue:
Reflections Of A Black & White Legend

I'm Les Bradd. I was born and bred in Buxton, Derbyshire on Bonfire Night 1947.

My mother told me in later years that the time was 7pm and as she looked out of the window from her maternity ward bed a rocket shot up into the night sky to be followed by my entrance to the world.

I was here and on this earth as a result of the large snowfall in February when snow drifts reached the bedroom windows of mum and dad's house.

For this reason, they were not able to get out of the house and so I believe most of the time was spent in a bed that led to my creation.

My mum and dad had moved from London to live in Buxton in 1937. Both came from working-class backgrounds and dad loved his football having played for Grays Athletic before getting a place in Buxton's team.

His full-time job was working as a train driver in a local limestone quarry and mum helped with added income by working as a cleaner in a Buxton store.

I was taught at an early age about right and wrong together with respect for other people and their property.

I was given many tasks by mum and dad in helping around the house and during my infant school years I learned very quickly how to look after myself and travelled on a three-mile bus ride to and from school on my own.

Dad was always around at weekends teaching me to play football and I really enjoyed many happy hours on the field.

Mum was often working on Saturdays and my older sister Margaret was given the task of looking after me. I did not see too much of my big brother Arthur as he is eleven years older than me and was enlisted for National Service before I was eight.

As I moved into secondary education, sport and in particular football became a big part of my life. After-school matches on the local park were hugely popular with many of the young boys from around the area and I learned many life skills from these games.

They would begin with small numbers probably three on each side and would finish when it was dark with probably fifteen on each team. The older boys would look after the younger, smaller ones and make sure no bullying took place.

As we grew up we had a clear understanding of how we should behave and show respect to others particularly those older than ourselves.

My dream was always to become a professional footballer but deep down I did not think it would happen.

It was a special treat to see a professional match as the nearest teams were in Manchester which is nearly 30 miles away from Buxton to the north or Derby which is over 30 miles to the south. Transport was not as it is today and I was lucky to see more than two games a season.

I loved local amateur football and after leaving school I got my place in a local village team from Earl Sterndale.

It was during my time there that I was offered a trial with Rotherham United and offered a full professional contract. I was only at Rotherham for a few months and moved to Nottingham to play for Notts County during which time I went on to play over four hundred games in a ten-year period and become the Club's all-time highest goal-scorer.

I had many battles with Nottingham Forest over the years and one game in particular stands out above the rest which I am sure has 'vivid' memories for the author of this book.

It was in 1975 at Forest's City Ground and the match was due to be shown on Star Soccer on ITV the following afternoon. With 89 minutes shown on the clock and the score at 0-0 with Forest in control of the game, our left-winger Ian Scanlan broke loose down the wing away from Viv Anderson and crossed a high ball into the penalty box around ten yards from goal.

The ball was just a little too high for Sammy Chapman – the Forest centre-half – and I rose to head the ball into the net. The referee had barely restarted the game when he blew the final whistle and we won the game 1-0 amid ecstatic scenes from the Notts County players and supporters.

My career lasted 18 years including spells with Stockport County, Wigan Athletic and Bristol Rovers after which I remained in Nottingham spending 12 years working for Notts County Football Club, raising funds through commercial activities before moving to Nottingham

Forest in 1994 to work as assistant to the commercial manager.

During my time at the Club I was involved in many fund-raising events covering football, golf and sporting dinners to name a few and I feel very privileged on one occasion to have been involved in arranging for Brian Clough to be the guest of honour at one of the best sporting dinners that was arranged by the Club.

It was a 25-year Celebration Dinner in 2004 to mark the anniversary of Forest winning the European Cup and it was staged at The East Midlands Conference Centre.

Brian was not on the best of terms with the Club following his departure as manager and I got my friend Ronnie Fenton to persuade Brian to attend with nearly all the playing squad to celebrate the victory in beating Hamburg in Madrid.

It was a fabulous evening during which all the players were interviewed to recall memories of the cup run after which Brian took centre stage with the microphone.

He talked for nearly half an hour about each player in a manner that belittled them beyond belief before putting each one at the top of a pedestal.

It was an amazing speech and the evening was concluded by having photographs with the sponsors that nearly didn't happen, as the players and the manager were starting to leave the room in all directions to make their way home. I eventually got them all together and we managed to get the relevant photos taken in a private room which was a great relief.

I suffered a heart attack within two weeks of the event and after speaking to various medical staff in the hospital it was thought that stress from the evening would have been a factor in bringing on my heart attack.

It was during my time at Forest in 1998 that I first came into contact with Paul Lowe who was assisting in providing education to youngsters with learning difficulties in the new Study Centre at The City Ground.

Many of the youngsters came from disadvantaged areas of Nottingham and some of whom could be disruptive at times.

He also worked with the 16-18 year old apprentice footballers in the Forest Academy. I did not know much about Paul other than he was 'Forest daft' and seldom missed a game and that he dedicated his spare time to raising funds for a charity that he formed by the name of SportActs that helped fund programmes for young people with various issues in life.

SportActs held many fund-raising sporting dinners and I managed to attend some excellent events but the one that stands out above others was the final dinner in 2008 at The Derek Randall Lounge at Trent Bridge.

Paul had decided that he needed a new challenge and put everything in place to move to Spain. So beforehand, he arranged a farewell dinner as a way of saying 'thank you' to everyone that had supported the charity over the years.

The event was well-attended and following an enjoyable three-course meal guests relaxed and listened to the guest speaker's memories of his times playing football and serving in the army during the Falklands War.

After the speaker had finished his presentation, the master of ceremonies for the evening introduced Paul to the audience to give his farewell speech to everyone.

I was astonished at what followed during the next fifteen minutes as Paul spoke very passionately about what he had achieved with SportActs. After a short space of time it was very clear though, he had drunk too much to be able to speak respectfully to an audience.

His language was colourful, to the point that a lot of the people that had supported the charity for several years – including many ladies – got up and left the room. The MC tried to take the microphone off Paul but to no avail.

Years of internal turmoil had finally come to a head and like a festering abscess – spectacularly burst.

Our paths did not cross for a while and it was not until 2012 that we met again by chance whilst I was working for a medical supply company. Paul had returned from Spain and told me that he had stopped drinking alcohol and founded a new charity by the name of Sporting HEARTS.

We had a cup of tea together and a chat in which he outlined his objectives to help youngsters stay out of trouble through sport and asked me if I would like to help and become an ambassador for his charity.

Paul had a very tough time in his early years growing up on the Bestwood Estate in Nottingham and I felt the passion in him and his desire to make life better for youngsters brought up in similar circumstances.

I had been the victim of burglary when my car was broken into at my home by a youngster and goods were stolen to exchange for drugs. I understood Paul's thoughts and he had already recruited my friend Paul Hart as President so I agreed to help and became an ambassador for Sporting HEARTS.

It has been an honour to have worked with Paul and Sporting HEARTS initially as an ambassador and then on its board of directors as President in the years that followed until he decided to close the charity in 2017.

I was able to see how Paul dedicated and channelled his time and energy in providing funding to organise a series of programmes in many communities that included boxing, cricket, football, cycling, running and much more to help thousands of children to enjoy a much better life whilst also improving the lives of many adults.

I was also able to witness his leadership skills in organising many successful fund-raising events as well as acquiring funding through careful grant applications.

Paul has applied his skills very successfully in helping and mentoring many people to get their lives back on track following setbacks.

Groups of young footballers at Notts County Football Club have listened to Paul's message and told me that they found the session to be inspirational and one that they should follow if they wish to achieve their goals in life.

Paul has been a great help to me during the twenty years that we have known each other and it goes without saying that he is a true friend.

Supporting HEARTS Global

'When we read that there are nearly 50,000 children in gangs, you could be forgiven for thinking that we were living in Dickensian England, not the 21st century. Yet they are among hundreds of thousands of children who are vulnerable or living in high-risk family situations'.

ANNE LONGFIELD OBE, CHILDREN'S COMMISSIONER, 2017

For example, there are more than 15,000 children with parents who have alcohol issues and almost 12,000 with parents being treated for drug problems. Children's Commissioner Anne Longfield OBE described the figures as 'shocking and very significant,' adding that they were 'just the tip of the iceberg'. So it's easy to imagine that these figures would go into the millions worldwide.

HEARTS Global (Community Interest Company) is an organisation dedicated to making a powerful, positive difference to communities locally, nationally and globally. This is achieved by providing a range of personal development related services that add outstanding value to individuals and communities; as well as reinvesting profits back into educational life-improving projects around the globe.

The CIC's predecessor, the Sporting HEARTS charity, provided a sporting chance in life to young people from disadvantaged communities within the UK. Since its formation in 2010, it has positively affected the lives of over 3,000 young people over a six-year period.

At HEARTS, we share Archbishop Desmond Tutu's message:

'It is our moral obligation to give every child the best education possible'.

We recognise that we can all give something, whether that is our time, resources or cash.

We are truly grateful for any donation and would be delighted to talk to you about the difference your gift will make. To donate to HEARTS Global, please go to:

http://www.heartsglobal.org

About The Author

Paul Lowe embraces HEARTS and inspires minds to help people achieve success in the game of life.

As an author, mentor, and inspirational speaker, Paul has an unswerving passion for facilitating positive transformation in the world.

He is a qualified ILM level-5 Business Coach, New Insights VIP Life Coach and Robbins Strategic Intervention Coach.

Paul now uses his diverse experiences to make a positive impact on the lives of individuals and communities – globally.

As the founder of the HEARTS Global brand, he is totally committed to the HEARTS vision of:

Helping Everyone Achieve Results Towards Success

If It's Meant To Be, It Will Show - If It's Not, Let It Go!

96862659R00083

Made in the USA
Columbia, SC
03 June 2018